Cover Up

with Nicky Epstein

Cover Up

with Nicky Epstein

sixth&spring books

sixth&spring books

Editorial Director
ELAINE SILVERSTEIN

Book Division Manager
ERICA SMITH

Associate Editor
AMANDA KEISER

Art Director
CHI LING MOY

Associate Art Director
SHEENA T. PAUL

Graphic Designer
MICHAEL YONG

Technical Illustrations
JANE FAY
ULI MÖNCH
MICHAEL YONG

Yarn Editor
TANIS GRAY

Bookings Manager
RACHAEL STEIN

Instructions Editor
SHIRI MOR

Instructions Checkers
RITA GREENFEDER
ROSEMARY DRYSDALE
EVE NG

Copy Editors
KRISTINA SIGLER
WENDY R. PRESTON

Photography
MARCUS TULLIS

Stylist
LAURA MAFFEO

Vice President, Publisher
TRISHA MALCOLM

Production Manager
DAVID JOINNIDES

Creative Director
JOE VIOR

President, Sixth&Spring Books
ART JOINNIDES

Library of Congress Control Number: 2007920929
ISBN: 1-933027-22-3
ISBN 13: 978-1-933027-22-7

1 3 5 7 9 10 8 6 4 2
Manufactured in China

First Edition

Introduction

Afghans: I love them! I love designing them; I love knitting them; I love giving them as gifts; I love having them around the house. They are perhaps the most enduring of all knitted pieces. They are warm, comforting, colorful, beautiful, and have myriad uses. They can become heirlooms. They embody love!

I am often asked how many afghans I've designed. Honestly, there have been so many over the years that I've lost count. Many of the knitting magazines and yarn companies that I designed them for have kept them, but somehow along the way I've managed to hold on to a few of my favorites. I am very happy to share my personal collection with you now.

Putting together this book has been a pleasant trip down memory lane. Each afghan has special memories attached to it: the wonderful people I've met over the years, the excitement and fufillment that I felt as I designed the afghans and watched them come to life, and the delight in seeing and hearing people appreciate them.

A note about the yarns I've chosen for this book: Yarns change over time, as yarn companies introduce new lines of yarn and new colors. For some of the afghans in this book, the original yarns or original colors are no longer available. However, I have personally selected readily available substitutes that will yield results that will equal or surpass my original design.

I hope you feel as much joy in making these pieces as I've felt in creating them. Whether you keep them or give them as gifts, I hope you feel the love!

Woodland Counterpane

In this afghan, traditional counterpanes are turned to form diamonds and sewn together in combination with stockinette-stitch colorwork diamonds. The edge is garter stitch with mitered corners. The rustic animal motifs are a unique complement to the classic counterpanes. Using traditional counterpanes in this unusual way makes the afghan a showstopper.

KNITTED MEASUREMENTS

52" x 78"/132cm x 198cm

MATERIALS

• 20 3½oz/100g balls (each approx 220yd/200m) of Reynolds/JCA, Inc. *Utopia* (100% acrylic) in #187 Maroon (A)
• 1 skein each in #35 Beige (B), #112 Tan (C), #73 Brown (D), #210 Light Blue (E), #77 Dark Blue (F), #75 Light Green (G), #303 Medium Green (H), #144 Dark Green (I), #74 Kelly Green (J), #30 Rust (K), #176 Gold (L), and #353 Gray (M)
• Size U.S. 8 (5mm) circular needle (used as a straight needle), at least 36"/91.5cm length OR SIZE TO OBTAIN GAUGE
• Yarn needle

GAUGE

18 sts and 26 rows = 4"/10cm over stockinette st.
TAKE TIME TO CHECK GAUGE.

SPECIAL STITCH

Make bobble–(K1, p1, k1, p1, k1) all into next st, turn, k5, turn, p5tog.

TRIANGLES

(make 72)
Using A, cast on 3 sts.
Row 1 P1, yo, k1, yo, p1.
Row 2 K2, p1, k2.
Row 3 (P1, yo) twice, k1, (yo, p1) twice.
Row 4 K3, p3, k3.
Row 5 P1, yo, p2, (k1, yo) twice, k1, p2, yo, p1.
Row 6 K4, p5, k4.
Row 7 P1, yo, p3, k2, yo, k1, yo, k2, p3, yo, p1.
Row 8 K5, p7, k5.
Row 9 P1, yo, p4, k3, yo, k1, yo, k3, p4, yo, p1.
Row 10 K6, p9, k6.
Row 11 P1, yo, p5, k4, yo, k1, yo, k4, p5, yo, p1.
Row 12 K7, p11, k7.
Row 13 P1, yo, p6, k5, yo, k1, yo, k5, p6, yo, p1.
Row 14 K8, p13, k8.
Row 15 P1, yo, p7, k6, yo, k1, yo, k6, p7, yo, p1.
Row 16 K9, p15, k9.
Row 17 P1, yo, p8, skp, k11, k2tog, p8, yo, p1.
Row 18 and all rem even rows K the k and yo sts, p the p sts.
Row 19 P1, yo, p9, skp, k9, k2tog, p9, yo, p1.
Row 21 P1, yo, p10, skp, k7, k2tog, p10, yo, p1.
Row 23 P1, yo, p11, skp, k5, k2tog, p11, yo, p1.
Row 25 P1, yo, p12, skp, k3, k2tog, p12, yo, p1.
Row 27 P1, yo, p13, skp, k1, k2tog, p13, yo, p1.
Row 29 P1, yo, p14, sk2p, p14, yo, p1.
Row 31 P1, yo, p31, yo, p1.
Row 33 P1, (yo, k2tog) 16 times, (yo, p1) twice.
Row 35 P1, (yo, k2tog) 17 times, (yo, p1) twice.
Row 37 P1, (yo, k2tog) 18 times, (yo, p1) twice.
Row 39 P1, yo, p39, yo, p1.

Row 41 P1, yo, p41, yo, p1.
Row 43 P1, yo, p3, (make bobble, p5) 6 times, make bobble, p3, yo, p1.
Row 45 P1, yo, p45, yo, p1.
Row 47 P1, yo, p47, yo, p1.
Bind off.

DIAMONDS

(make 6)
Using A, cast on 3 sts.
Working in stockinette st, inc 1 st at beg of every row until you have 71 sts.
Dec 1 st at beg of every row until you have 3 sts again.
Bind off.

EMBROIDERY

Work in duplicate st, working 1 chart on each of 6 diamonds.

FINISHING

Assembly

Sew triangles and diamonds together as shown in diagram.

Border

Using A and with RS facing, pick up and k 290 sts across top edge.
Working in garter st, inc 1 st at each end of needle every other row 3 times—296 sts.
Continue evenly until border measures 1".
Bind off.
Work bottom edge the same.
Using A and with RS facing, pick up and k 378 sts along one side edge, and work same as top border.
Work other side edge the same.
Sew mitered corners together. Weave in all loose ends.

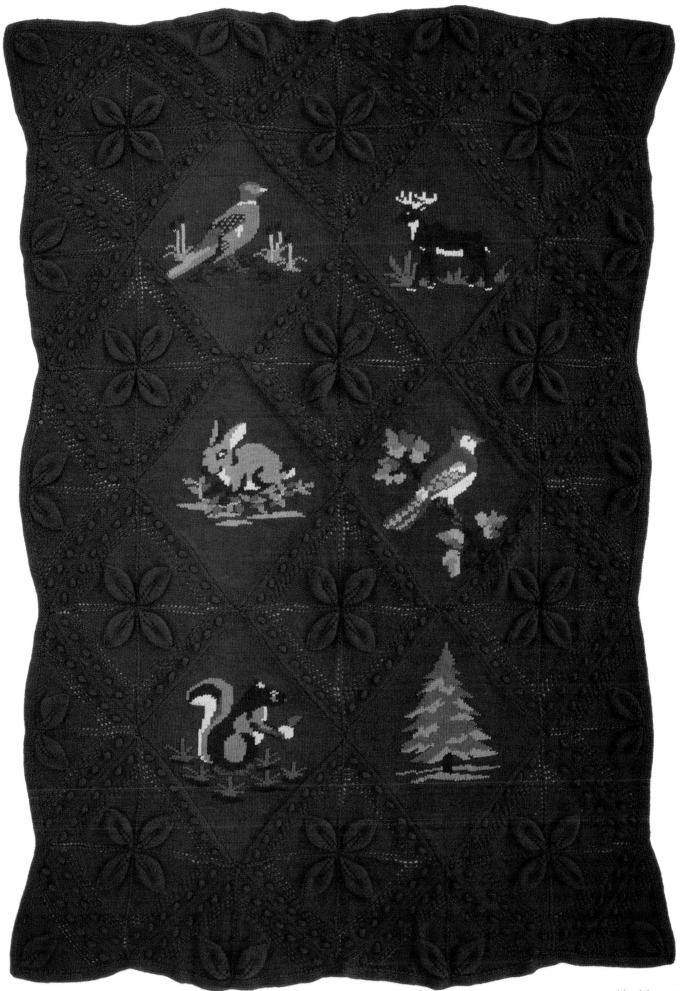

ASSEMBLY DIAGRAM

PHEASANT	REINDEER
BUNNY	BLUE JAY
SQUIRREL	TREE

PHEASANT

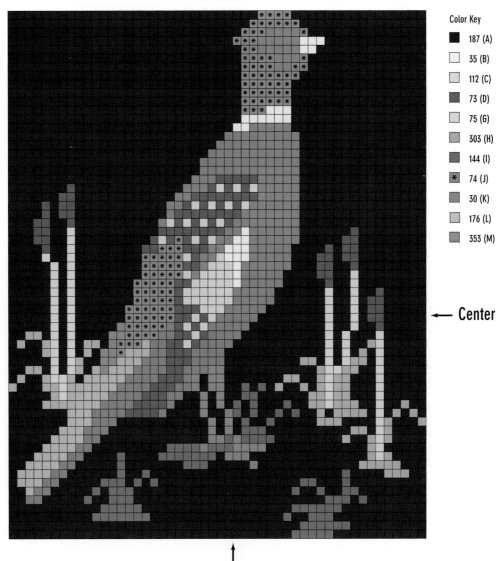

Color Key

- ■ 187 (A)
- □ 35 (B)
- ▨ 112 (C)
- ■ 73 (D)
- □ 75 (G)
- ▨ 303 (H)
- ■ 144 (I)
- ✳ 74 (J)
- ■ 30 (K)
- ▨ 176 (L)
- ■ 353 (M)

← Center

↑
Center

REINDEER

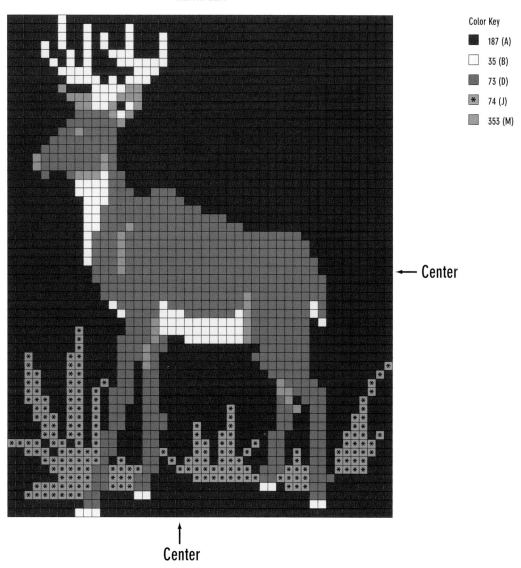

Color Key

■	187 (A)
□	35 (B)
▨	73 (D)
✳	74 (J)
▧	353 (M)

← Center

↑
Center

BUNNY

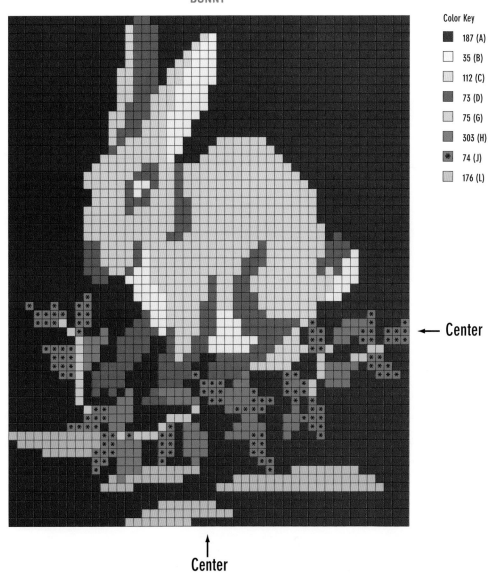

Color Key
- 187 (A)
- 35 (B)
- 112 (C)
- 73 (D)
- 75 (G)
- 303 (H)
- 74 (J)
- 176 (L)

← Center

↑
Center

BLUE JAY

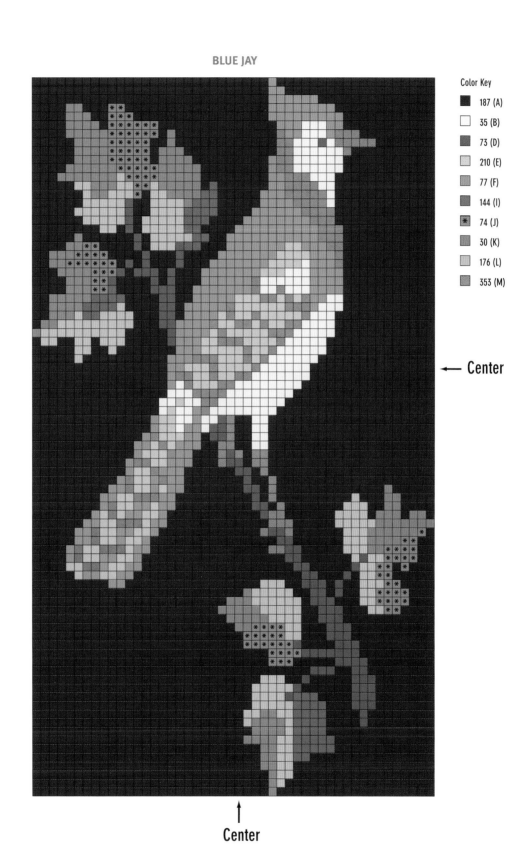

Color Key

■ 187 (A)
□ 35 (B)
■ 73 (D)
■ 210 (E)
■ 77 (F)
■ 144 (I)
※ 74 (J)
■ 30 (K)
■ 176 (L)
■ 353 (M)

← Center

↑
Center

SQUIRREL

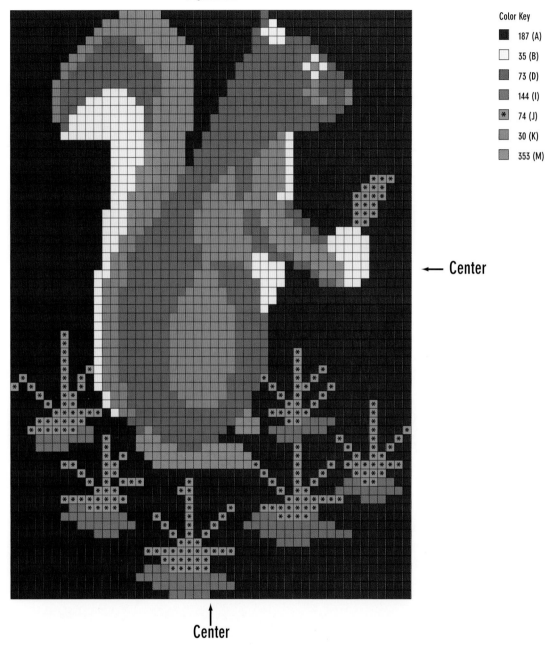

Color Key

- ■ 187 (A)
- □ 35 (B)
- ■ 73 (D)
- ■ 144 (I)
- ✳ 74 (J)
- ■ 30 (K)
- ■ 353 (M)

← Center

↑
Center

TREE

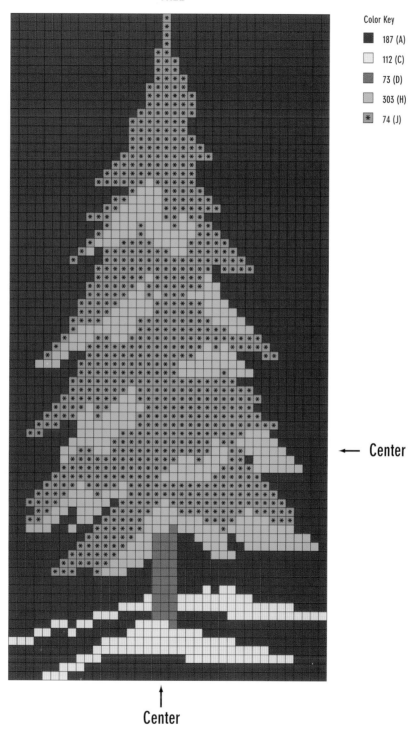

Color Key
- 187 (A)
- 112 (C)
- 73 (D)
- 303 (H)
- 74 (J)

← **Center**

↑
Center

Doves

Included here are many of my signature design elements, with motif colorwork as the central focus and extensive embroidery embellishments. Note how the feather-lace frame is broken to allow the motif to flow over each side. To finish the piece I used a vintage lace edge stitch and mitered the corners. The colors I selected evoke the palette of the Victorian era.

40" x 50"/101.5cm x 127cm

MATERIALS

- 15 1¾ oz/50 gm skeins (each approx 137 yd/127 m) of RYC/Westminster Fibers, Inc. *Pure Wool DK* (100% superwash wool) in #024 Petal (A)
- 1 skein each in #013 Enamel (C), #014 Hay (D), #016 Hessian (E), #017 Mocha (F), #023 Shamrock (G), #022 Emerald (H), #020 Parsley (I), #039 Lavender (J), #009 Ultramarine (K), #006 Pier (L), #034 Spice (M), #028 Raspberry (N), #025 Tea Rose (O), and #029 Pomegranate (P)
- 1 1¾ oz/50 gm skeins (each approx 100 yd/109 m) of RYC/Westminster Fibers, Inc. *Silk/Wool DK* (50% merino wool, 50% silk) in #00301 Limewash (B)
- Size U.S. 6 (4mm) circular needle (used as a straight needle), at least 36" length OR SIZE TO OBTAIN GAUGE
- Yarn needle

GAUGE

22 sts and 30 rows = 4"/10cm over stockinette st.
TAKE TIME TO CHECK GAUGE.

FISHTAIL LACE PANEL PATTERN

(11 sts)

Row 1 P1, k1, yo, k2, sk2p, k2, yo, k1, p1.

Row 2 K1, p9, k1.

Row 3 P1, k2, yo, k1, sk2p, k1, yo, k2, p1.

Row 4 As row 2.

Row 5 P1, k3, yo, sk2p, yo, k3, p1.

Row 6 As row 2.

Rep rows 1–6 for fishtail lace panel pat.

FISHTAIL BORDER PATTERN

(multiple of 8 sts + 1)

Row 1 K1*, yo, k2, sk2p, k2, yo, k1*.

Row 2 Purl.

Row 3 K2*, yo, k1, sk2p, k1, yo, k3*; rep to last 7 st, yo, k1, sk2p, k1, yo, k2.

Row 4 Purl.

Row 5 K3*, yo, sk2p, yo, k5; rep to last 6 st, yo, sk2p, yo, k3*.

Row 6 Purl.

Rep rows 1–6 for fishtail border pat.

CENTER PANEL

Using A, cast on 164 sts, and work in stockinette st for 4"/10cm, ending on a RS row.

Next row P40, inc 5 sts evenly over next 84 sts, p40—169 sts.

Begin lace patterns as foll:

Next row K29, work 11 sts in fishtail lace panel pat, work 89 sts in fishtail border pat, work 11 sts in fishtail panel pat, k29.

Cont in pats as established for 11 more rows, dec 5 sts evenly over center 89 sts on last row—164 sts.

Next row K29, work 11 sts in fishtail lace panel pat, k84, work 11 sts in fishtail lace panel pat, k29.

Cont in stockinette st and fishtail lace panel pat for 17 more rows.

Beg working color chart in intarsia on center stockinette st panel. When color chart and fishtail lace panel overlap, work color chart only, eliminating fishtail lace panel, and restoring it when possible.

Using A only, work 16 more rows in stockinette st and fishtail lace panel pat after chart.

Work top lace border same as bottom.

Cont in stockinette st only for 4"/10cm more. Bind off.

EMBROIDERY

See chart for placement.

Flowers Work lazy daisy sts using L. Center daisy st with a 3-wrap French knot using M.

Leaf veins Split green yarns into 2 plies, and work stem st.

Basket Work trellis st using F.

Birds' eyes Work French knot using F.

FINISHING

Border (make 4 pieces)

Using A, cast on 26 sts.

Row 1 K2tog, k1, yo, k2tog, k5, k2tog, yo, k2tog, k9, yo, k2tog, k1—24 sts.

Row 2 Sl1, k2, yo, k2tog, k1, k2tog, (yo, k2tog) twice, k2, yo, k2tog, k3, k2tog, yo, k3—23 sts.

Row 3 Yo, k4, yo, k2tog, k1, k2tog, yo, k11, yo, k2tog, k1—24 sts.

Row 4 Sl1, k2, yo, k2tog, k3, (yo, k2tog) twice, k3, yo, sk2p, yo, k6—24 sts.

Row 5 Yo, k1, k2tog, yo twice, k18, yo, k2tog, k1—26 sts.

Row 6 Sl1, k2, yo, k2tog, k4, (yo, k2tog) twice, k8, (k1, p1) in double yo of previous row, k3—26 sts.

Row 7 K1, k2tog, * yo twice, k2tog; rep from * once more, k16, yo, k2tog, k1—27 sts.

Row 8 Sl1, k2, yo, k2tog, k5, (yo, k2tog) twice, k6, * (k1, p1) in double yo of previous row, k1; rep from * once more, k1—27 sts.

Row 9 K2tog, k1, k2tog, yo twice, k2tog, k3, yo,

k1, yo, k2tog, k11, yo, k2tog, k1—27 sts.

Row 10 Sl1, k2, yo, k2tog, k3, k2tog, yo, k2tog, (yo, k3) twice, yo, k2tog, k2, (k1, p1) in double yo of previous row, k2tog, k1—27 sts.

Row 11 K2tog, k3, k2tog, yo, k5, yo, k2tog, k10, yo, k2tog, k1—26 sts.

Row 12 Sl1, k2, yo, k2tog, k2, (k2tog, yo) twice, k3, yo, k7, yo, k2tog, k1, k2tog—26 sts.

Rep rows 1–12 29 more times for 2 pieces, and 32 more times for rem 2 pieces.

Bind off.

Sew short lace panels to top and bottom of center panel, and long lace panels to side edges, leaving 1¼" of each panel unattached at either side. Sew corners together. Using yarn needle, gather unattached portion of lace panel, and fasten off corner.

Block edging flat.

Weave in all loose ends.

CENTER PANEL (BOTTOM)

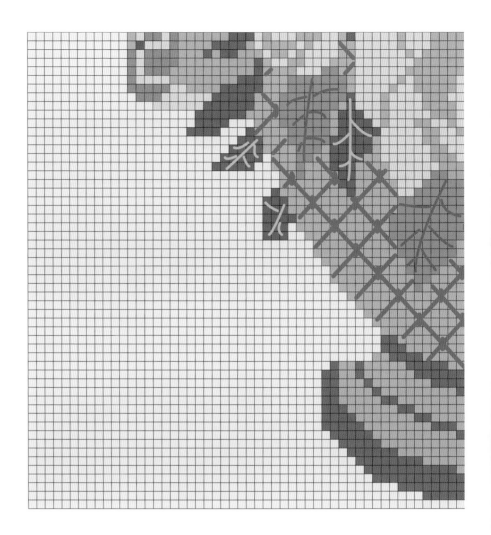

FISHTAIL BORDER

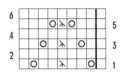

8 + 1 sts

FISHTAIL PANEL

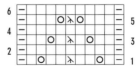

11 sts

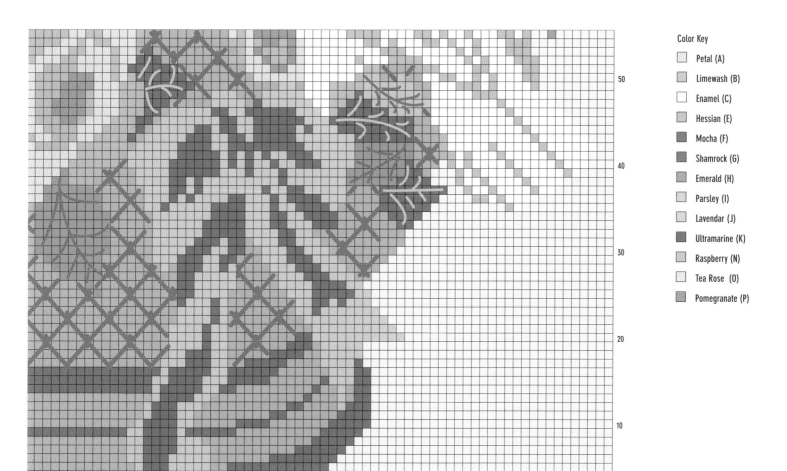

50

40

30

20

10

1

122 sts

LACE BORDER

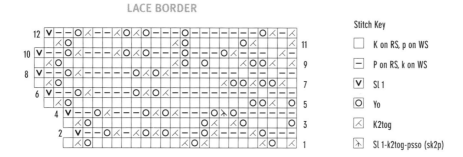

Stitch Key

K on RS, p on WS

P on RS, k on WS

Sl 1

Yo

K2tog

Sl 1-k2tog-psso (sk2p)

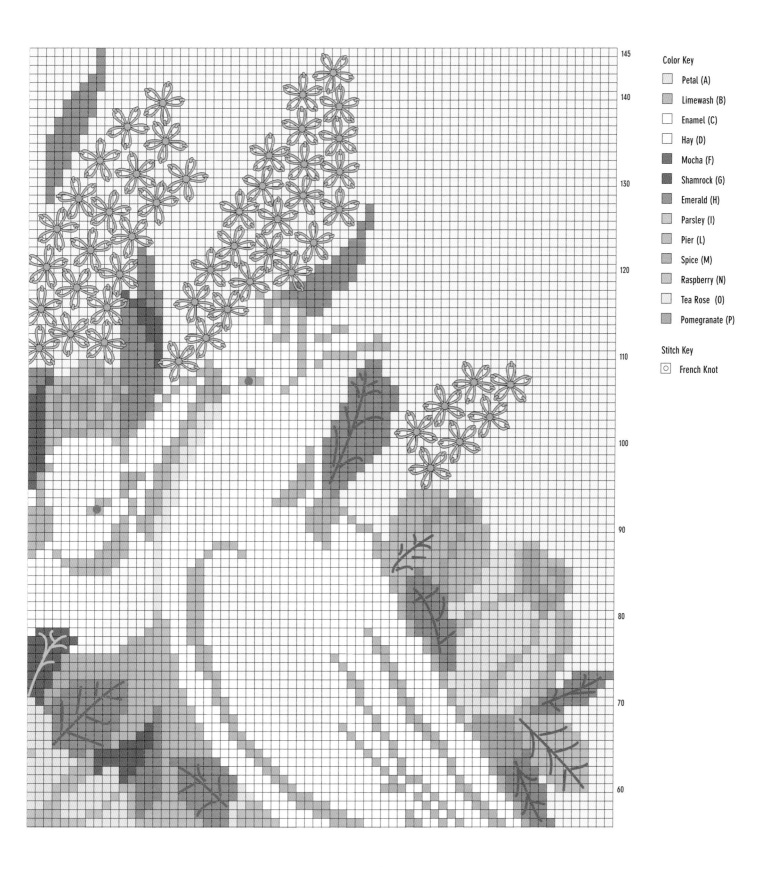

145
140
130
120
110
100
90
80
70
60

Color Key

- ☐ Petal (A)
- ☐ Limewash (B)
- ☐ Enamel (C)
- ☐ Hay (D)
- ☐ Mocha (F)
- ☐ Shamrock (G)
- ☐ Emerald (H)
- ☐ Parsley (I)
- ☐ Pier (L)
- ☐ Spice (M)
- ☐ Raspberry (N)
- ☐ Tea Rose (O)
- ☐ Pomegranate (P)

Stitch Key

- ⊙ French Knot

English Garden

The floral still life is worked in intarsia; the afghan has a double border of mitered stockinette stitch sewn onto a mitered lace border. I still have the original hand-drawn chart that I made for this piece. As I knit the afghan, my husband, Howard, read each line of the chart to me—and simultaneously watched ball games!

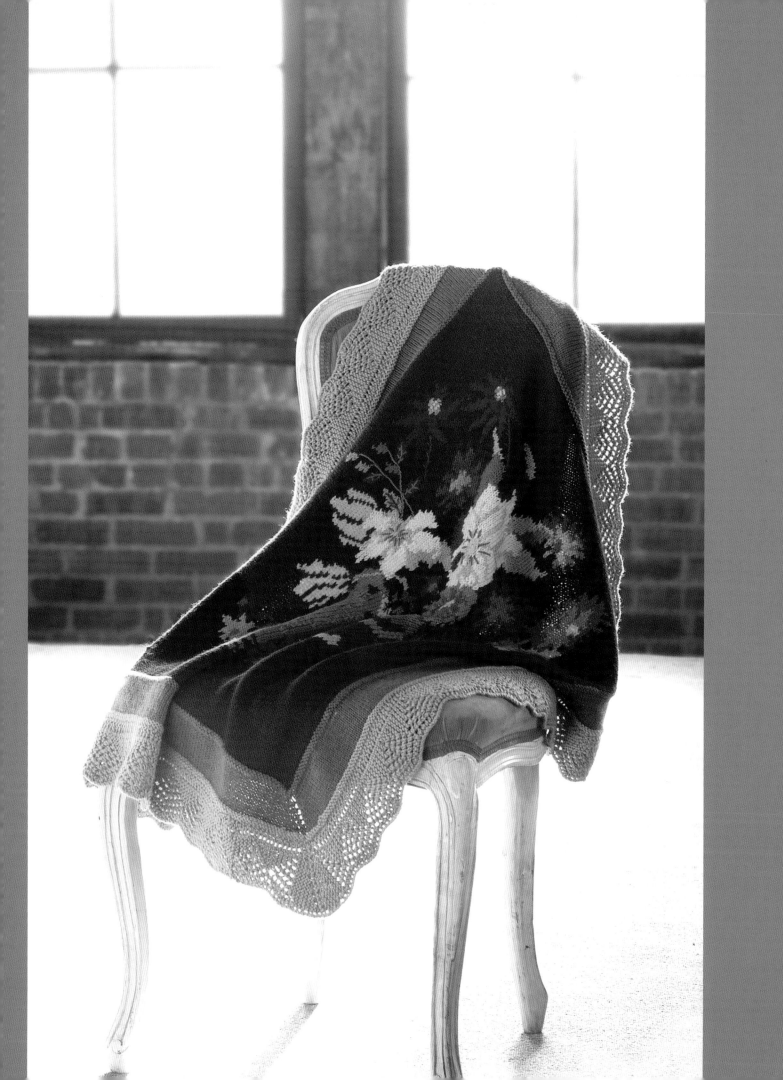

KNITTED MEASUREMENTS

• 30" x 38"/76cm x 96cm

MATERIALS

• 5 100 oz/50g skeins (each approx 137yd/125m) RYC/Westminster Fibers, Inc. *Pure Wool DK* (100% super wash wool) in #014 Hay (AA)
• 2 skeins in #016 Hessian (B) and #017 Mocha (Z)
• 1 skein in #037 Port (A), #025 Tea Rose (C), #011 Navy (D), #006 Pier (E), #007 Cypress (F), #041 Scarlet (G), #029 Pomegranate (H), #015 Barley (I), #024 Petal (J), #021 Glade (K), #022 Emerald (L), #023 Shamrock (M), #020 Parsley (N), #035 Quarry (O), #034 Spice (P), #008 Marine (Q), #040 Tangerine (R), #005 Glacier (S), #032 Gilt (T), #036 Kiss (U), #028 Raspberry (V), #030 Damson (W) #039 Lavender (X), #026 Hyacinth (Y)
• Size U.S. 5 (3.75mm) needles OR SIZE TO OBTAIN GAUGE
• Yarn bobbins
• Yarn needles

GAUGE

21 sts and 28 rows = 4"/10cm over stockinette st.
TAKE TIME TO CHECK GAUGE.

BORDER LACE PATTERN

(14 sts)

Row 1 (WS) K2, yo, k2tog, k5, yo, k2tog, yo, k3—15 sts.

Row 2 and all even rows K1, yo, k2tog, k to end.

Row 3 K2, yo, k2tog, k4, (yo, k2tog) twice, yo, k3—16 sts.

Row 5 K2, yo, k2tog, k3, (yo, k2tog) 3 times, yo, k3—17 sts.

Row 7 K2, yo, k2tog, k2, (yo, k2tog) 4 times, yo, k3—18 sts.

Row 9 K2, yo, k2tog, k1, (yo, k2tog) 5 times, yo, k3—19 sts.

Row 11 K2, yo, k2tog, k1, k2tog, (yo, k2tog) 5 times, k2—18 sts.

Row 13 K2, yo, k2tog, k2, k2tog, (yo, k2tog) 4 times, k2—17 sts.

Row 15 K2, yo, k2tog, k3, k2tog, (yo, k2tog) 3 times, k2—16 sts.

Row 17 K2, yo, k2tog, k4, k2tog, (yo, k2tog) twice, k2—15 sts.

Row 19 K2, yo, k2tog, k5, k2tog, yo, k2tog, k2—14 sts.

Row 20 As row 2.

CENTER PANEL

Using A, cast on 107 sts. Work color chart in intarsia over center 105 sts, knitting the selvage sts on each row.
Work 12 more rows using Z only.
Bind off.

EMBROIDERY

Stems Using colors as shown, work stem st.
Leaf veins Using colors as shown, work stem st for center veins and straight st for short veins.

Pink flowers Using Y, work straight st.
Blue flowers Split T, use one strand to work straight st at bottom of flowers.
Red flowers Using T, work French knots at center of flowers.
Pansies Split X, and use one strand to work straight st at yellow center of flowers.

FINISHING

Inner border—short edges
(make 2)
Using B, cast on 121 sts. Knit 1 row, then purl one row.
Next 2 rows:
Row 1 (WS) Purl
Row 2 K2, yo, sk2p, k to last 5 sts, k3tog, yo, k2.
Rep rows 1 and 2 5 more times—109 sts.
Purl one row, knit 2 rows, then bind off.

Inner border—long edges
(make 2)
Using AA, cast on 156 sts, and work same as short edges—144 sts.
Bind off.

Outer border
Using AA, cast on 14 sts.
Work border lace pat once, then rep rows 1–9 only once more.
Turn corner.
Next 4 rows:
Row 1 (RS) K1, yo, k2tog, k to last 5 sts, sl1, turn work.
Row 2 K to end.
Row 3 K1, yo, k2tog, k to last 7 sts, sl1, turn work.

Row 4 K to end.

Cont in this manner, working 2 less sts at end of every other row 4 more times, then 1 less st once. End on a WS row.

Next 4 rows:

Row 1 (RS) K1, yo, k2tog, sl1, turn work.

Row 2 K to end.

Row 3 K1, yo, k2tog, k1, sl1, turn work.

Row 4 K to end.

Cont in this manner, working 2 more sts at end of every other row 5 more times.

Beg with row 10, work 20 rows of border lace pat 15 times (long edge), then turn corner as before.

Beg with row 10, work 20 rows of border lace pat 12 times (short edge), then turn corner as before.

Beg with row 10, work 20 rows of border lace pat 15 times (long edge), then turn corner as before.

Beg with row 10, work 20 rows of border lace pat 10 times, then work rows 10–19 once more.

Bind off. Sew together cast on and bound-off edges (short edge).

Assembly Sew bound-off edges of 4 pieces of inner border to center panel. Sew corners together. Sew straight edge of outer border around perimeter of piece.

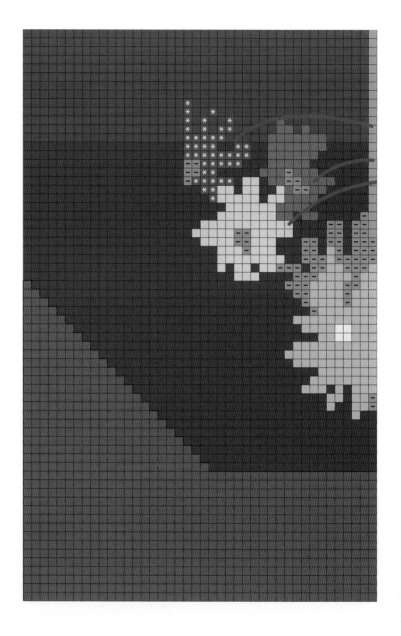

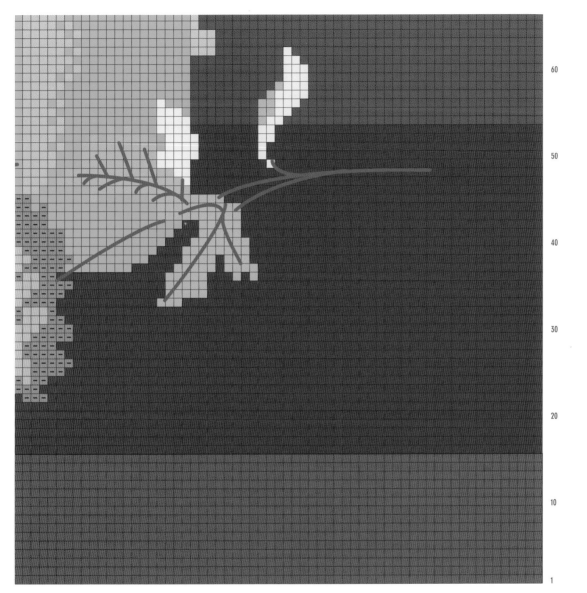

#037 Port (A)

#016 Hessian (B)

#007 Cypress (F)

#015 Barley (I)

#022 Emerald (L)

#023 Shamrock (M)

#020 Parsley (N)

#035 Quarry (O)

#034 Spice (P)

#040 Tangerine (R)

#005 Glacier (S)

#032 Gilt (T)

#030 Damson (W)

#017 Mocha (Z)

60

50

40

30

20

10

1

105 sts

CENTER PANEL (TOP)

Color Key

- ■ #037 Port (A)
- ⊟ #016 Hessian (B)
- ☐ #025 Tea Rose (C)
- ■ #011 Navy (D)
- ☐ #006 Pier (E)
- ▨ #007 Cypress (F)
- ■ #041 Scarlet (G)
- ✳ #029 Pomegranate (H)
- ▨ #015 Barley (I)
- ☐ #024 Petal (J)
- ■ #021 Glade (K)
- ▨ #022 Emerald (L)
- ✳ #023 Shamrock (M)
- ▨ #020 Parsley (N)
- ✳ #035 Quarry (O)
- ▨ #034 Spice (P)
- ⊟ #008 Marine (Q)
- ▨ #040 Tangerine (R)
- ▨ #005 Glacier (S)
- ☐ #032 Gilt (T)
- ⊟ #036 Kiss (U)
- ▨ #028 Raspberry (V)
- ■ #030 Damson (W)
- ▨ #039 Lavender (X)
- ▨ #026 Hyacinth (Y)
- ■ #017 Mocha (Z)

Stitch Key

- ☐ French Knot

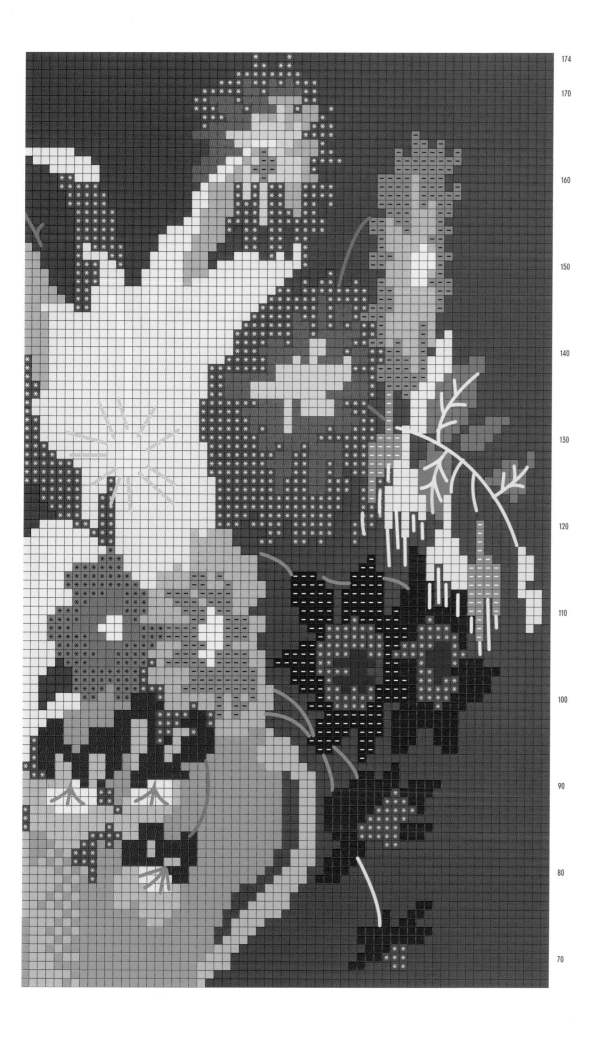

174
170
160
150
140
130
120
110
100
90
80
70

Liberty Bell

The motifs in this afghan are all-American. They are worked in horizontal intarsia repeats and separated with striping in easy textural knit stitches. The border is garter stitch, and each corner has a tassel attached.

KNITTED MEASUREMENTS

44" x 64"/106.5cm x 162.5cm

MATERIALS

• 3 3½oz/100g balls (each approx 220yd/201m) of Reynolds/JCA, Inc. *Signature* (80% acrylic, 20% wool) each in #67 Port (A), #10 Cream (B), #55 Blue (C), #81 Gray (D), and #21 Gold (E)
• 1 ball in #71 Brown (F)
• 1 skein of DMC *Embroidery Floss 117* (100% cotton) in #310 Black (G)
• Size U.S. 8 (5mm) circular needle (used as a straight needle), at least 36"/91.5cm length OR SIZE TO OBTAIN GAUGE
• Yarn needle

GAUGE

18 sts and 24 rows = 4"/10cm over stockinette st.
TAKE TIME TO CHECK GAUGE.

AFGHAN

Using C, cast on 198 sts, and work 14 rows in garter st.

NEXT 12 ROWS:

Row 1 (RS) Using C, k9, using A, k to last 9, using C, k9.

Rows 2 and 3 As row 1.

Row 4 Using C, k9, using B, p to last 9, using C, k9.

Rows 5–7 Using C, k9, using B, k to last 9, using C, k9.

Row 8 Using C, k9, using A, p to last 9, using C, k9.

Rows 9–11 Using C, k9, using A, k to last 9, using C, k9.

Row 12 (WS) Using C, k9, using B, p5 * work 25 sts of bell chart, using B, p4; rep from * 5 more times, using B, p1, using C, k9.

Cont as est by row 12 until bell chart is complete.

Next row (RS) Using C, k9, * work 7 sts of border chart 2; rep from * to last 14 sts, work 1st 5 sts of border chart 2 again, using C, k9.

Cont as est until border chart 2 is complete.

Next row (RS) Using C, k9, using D, k13, * work 28 sts of emblem chart, using D, k14; rep from * twice more, work 28 sts of emblem chart, using D, k13, using C, k9.

Cont as est until emblem chart is complete.

Next row (RS) Using C, k9, * work 6 sts of border chart 1; rep from * to last 9 sts, using C, k9.

Cont as est until border chart 1 is complete.

Next row (WS) Using C, k9, * work 30 sts of star chart; rep from * to last 9 sts, using C, k9.

Cont as est until star chart is complete.

NEXT 9 ROWS:

Row 1 (RS) Using C, k9, using B, k to last 9 sts, using C, k9.

Row 2 As row 1.

Row 3 Using C, k9, using F, k to last 9 sts, using C, k9.

Rows 4–6 Using C, k9, using F, p to last 9 sts, using C, k9.

Rows 7 and 8 As row 1.

Row 9 (RS) Using C, k9, using A, k3, * work 24 sts of eagle chart, using A, k6, rep from * 4 more times, work 24 sts of eagle chart, using A, k3, using C, k9.

Cont as est by row 9 until eagle chart is complete.

NEXT 9 ROWS:

Row 1 (RS) Using C, k9, using B, k to last 9 sts, using C, k9.

Row 2 As row 1.

Row 3 Using C, k9, using F, k to last 9 sts, using C, k9.

Rows 4–6 Using C, k9, using F, p to last 9 sts, using C, k9.

Rows 7 and 8 As row 1.

Row 9 (RS) Using C, k9, * work 30 sts of star chart; rep from * to last 9 sts, using C, k9.

Cont as est by row 9 until star chart is complete.

Next row (WS) Using C, k9, * work 6 sts of border chart 1; rep from * to last 9 sts, using C, k9.

Cont as est until border chart 1 is complete.

Next row (RS) Using C, k9, using D, k13, * work 28 sts of emblem chart, using D, k14; rep from * twice more, work 28 sts of emblem chart, using

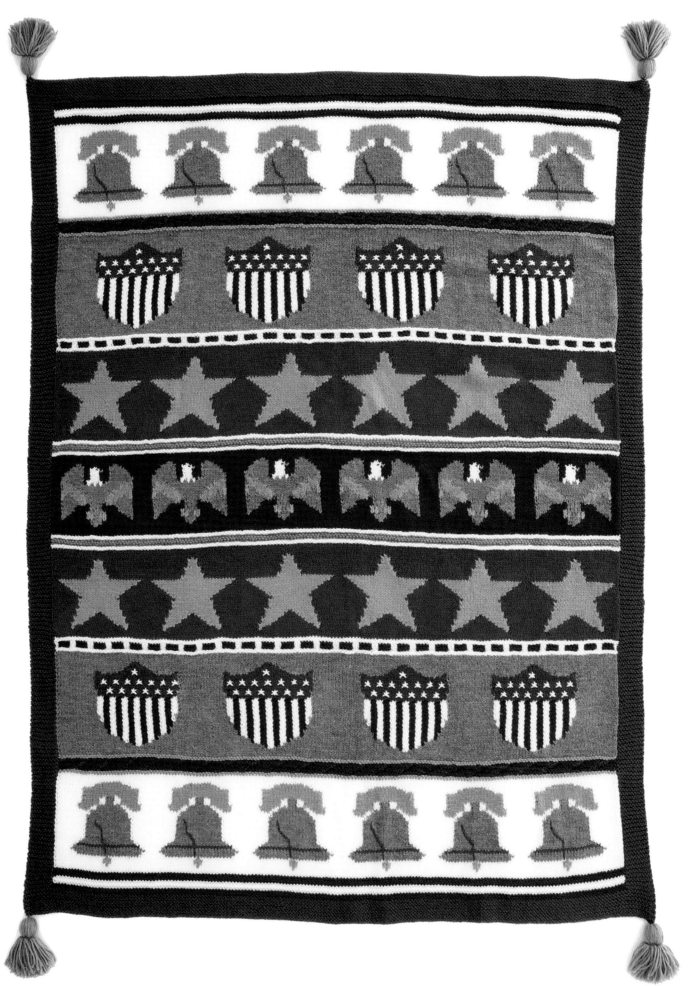

D, k13, using C, k9.

Cont as est until emblem chart is complete.

Next row (RS) Using C, k9, * work 7 sts of border chart 2; rep from * to last 14 sts, work 1st 5 sts of border chart 2 again, using C, k9.

Cont as est until border chart 2 is complete.

Next row (RS) Using C, k9, using B, k5 * work 25 sts of bell chart, using B, k4; rep from * 5 more times, using B, k1, using C, k9.

Cont as est until bell chart is complete.

NEXT 11 ROWS:

Row 1 (WS) Using C, k9, using A, p to last 9 sts, using C, k9.

Rows 2 and 3 As row 1.

Row 4 Using C, k9, using A, k to last 9 sts, using C, k9.

Row 5 Using C, k9, using B, p to last 9 sts, using C, k9.

Rows 6–8 Using C, k9, using B, k to last 9 sts, using C, k9.

Row 9 As row 1.

Rows 10 and 11 As row 4.

Using A only, work 14 rows in garter st.

Bind off.

EMBROIDERY

Using G, work in stem st for bell crack and eagles' eyes.

Using B, work in straight st for stars on emblem.

FINISHING

Tassels Using E, make 4 large tassels and attach at corners. To make tassel: Wrap yarn approx 60 times around a 9"/23cm-wide piece of cardboard. Insert an 18"/46cm-long piece of yarn at upper edge of cardboard. Pull tightly and knot securely near strands. Cut yarn loops at the base of the tassel. Wrap a 12"/30.5cm-long piece of yarn tightly around loops 1½"/3.5cm below top knot to form tassel neck. Knot securely, thread ends onto tapestry needle and pull ends to center of tassel. Trim tassel ends evenly.

BELL

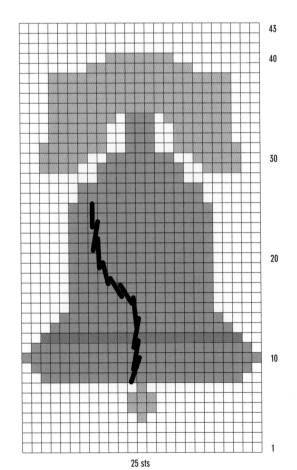

25 sts

BORDER

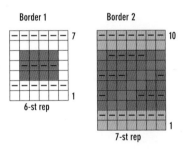

Border 1

7

1

6-st rep

Border 2

10

1

7-st rep

Color Key

■ Brick red (A)

□ White (B)

■ Blue (C)

■ Gray (D)

■ Gold (E)

■ Brown (F)Brown (F)

Stitch Key

− P on RS, k on WS with matching color
All other squares are k on RS, p on WS

EAGLE

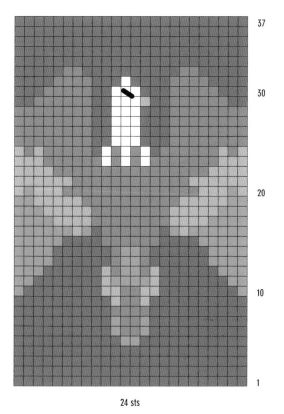

37

30

20

10

1

24 sts

STAR

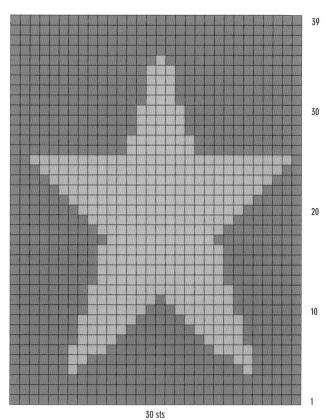

39

30

20

10

1

30 sts

EMBLEM

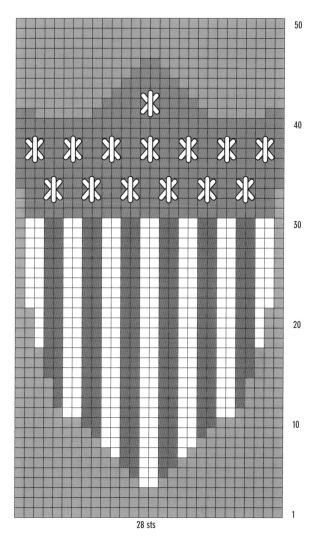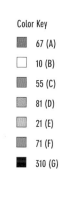

50

40

30

20

10

1

28 sts

Color Key

▨	67 (A)
☐	10 (B)
▨	55 (C)
▨	81 (D)
▨	21 (E)
▨	71 (F)
■	310 (G)

cover up with nicky epstein 39

Patchwork Floral

This is a good example of a piece that looks complicated but is in fact easy to make. The afghan background is worked in stockinette strips that change colors in combination to make squares. The florettes are made using a very simple cast-on/bind-off technique and are sewn to each square. The edge is interesting in that the bottom fringe is made using the same technique as the flowers and plays off the color changes in each square. The sides are worked in garter stitch, using a different color for each square.

KNITTED MEASUREMENTS

40" x 54"/101.5cm x 137cm,
including fringe

MATERIALS

• 3 3.5oz/100g skeins (each approx
183yd/169m) of Tahki
Yarns/Tahki•Stacy Charles, Inc.,
Donegal Tweed (100% pure new
wool) in #843 Blue (A),
#896 Purple (B),
#810 Pink (C), #874 Dark Red (D),
#832 Red (E), #893 orange (F),
894 Dark Green (G) and
#803 Green (H).
• Size U.S. 7 (4mm) circular needle
(for flowers, borders, and fringe) at
least 36" length (used as a straight
needle).
• Size U.S. 8 (4.5mm) needles (for
panels) OR SIZE TO OBTAIN GAUGE

GAUGE

18 sts and 28 rows = 4"/10cm over
stockinette st using larger needles.
TAKE TIME TO CHECK GAUGE.

REVERSE STOCKINETTE ST

All **RS** rows Purl.
All **WS** rows Knit.

PANEL 1 (Right)

Using C and larger needles, cast on 29 sts, and
work in stockinette st for 44 rows, beg with a
RS row.
Change to E, and work 44 rows in stockinette st.
Change to H, knit 1 row, then work 44 rows in
reverse stockinette st.
Change to B, purl 1 row, then work 44 rows in
stockinette st.
Change to F, and work 44 rows in stockinette st.
Change to D, and work 44 rows in stockinette st.
Change to G, knit 1 row, then work 44 rows in
reverse stockinette st.
Change to A, purl 1 row, then work 44 rows in
stockinette st. Bind off.

PANEL 2

Using D and larger needles, cast on 29 sts, and
work in reverse stockinette st for 45 rows, beg
with a WS row.
Change to F, and work 44 rows in stockinette st.
Change to A, and work 44 rows in stockinette st.
Change to E, knit 1 row, then work 44 rows in
reverse stockinette st.
Change to G, purl 1 row, then work 44 rows in
stockinette st.
Change to H, and work 44 rows in
stockinette st.
Change to B, and work 44 rows in stockinette st.
Change to C, knit 1 row, then work 44 rows in
reverse stockinette st. Bind off.

PANEL 3

Using H and larger needles, cast on 29 sts, and
work in stockinette st for 44 rows, beg with a
RS row.
Change to B, knit 1 row, then work 44 rows in
reverse stockinette st.
Change to C, purl 1 row, then work 44 rows in
stockinette st.
Change to D, and work 44 rows in stockinette st.
Change to A, and work 44 rows in stockinette st.
Change to E, knit 1 row, then work 44 rows in
reverse stockinette st.
Change to F, purl 1 row, then work 44 rows in
stockinette st.
Change to G, and work 44 rows in stockinette st.
Bind off.

PANEL 4

Using A and larger needles, cast on 29 sts, and
work in stockinette st for 44 rows, beg with a RS
row.
Change to E, and work 44 rows in stockinette st.
Change to H, knit 1 row, then work 44 rows in
reverse stockinette st.
Change to F, purl 1 row, then work 44 rows in
stockinette st.
Change to B, knit 1 row, then work 44 rows in
reverse stockinette st.
Change to G, purl 1 row, then work 44 rows in
stockinette st.
Change to C, and work 44 rows in stockinette st.
Change to D, knit 1 row, then work 44 rows in
reverse stockinette st. Bind off.

PANEL 5

Using F and larger needles, cast on 29 sts, and work in reverse stockinette st for 45 rows, beg with a WS row.

Change to D, and work 44 rows in stockinette st.

Change to G, and work 44 rows in stockinette st.

Change to A, knit 1 row, then work 44 rows in reverse stockinette st.

Change to C, purl 1 row, then work 44 rows in stockinette st.

Change to B, and work 44 rows in stockinette st.

Change to H, and work 44 rows in stockinette st.

Change to E, knit 1 row, then work 44 rows in reverse stockinette st. Bind off.

PANEL 6

Using G and larger needles, cast on 29 sts, and work in stockinette st for 44 rows, beg with a RS row.

Change to C, knit 1 row, then work 44 rows in reverse stockinette st.

Change to B, purl 1 row, then work 44 rows in stockinette st.

Change to H, and work 44 rows in stockinette st.

Change to E, and work 44 rows in stockinette st.

Change to F, knit 1 row, then work 44 rows in reverse stockinette st.

Change to A, purl 1 row, then work 44 rows in stockinette st.

Change to C, and work 44 rows in stockinette st. Bind off.

FLOWERS

(make 8 using A, 6 using B, 5 using C, 4 using D, 7 using E, 8 using F, 4 using G, and 6 using H) Using smaller needle, cast on 12 sts.

Rows 1 and 2 Knit.

Row 3 Bind off 10 sts, k to end—2 sts.

Row 4 K2, then cast on 10 sts using the cable cast on—12 sts.

Rows 5 and 6 Knit.

Row 7 As row 3.

Rep rows 4–7 5 more times—7 flower petals. Bind off. Sew together cast-on and bound-off edges to form a circle.

FINISHING

Assembly Sew panels together, and sew flowers onto color squares as indicated in picture.

Border Using H and smaller needle and with RS facing, pick up and k 35 sts along right edge of pink block, join B and pick up and k 35 sts along edge of red block, join F and pick up and k 35 sts along edge of green block, join G and pick up and k 35 sts along edge of purple block, join D and pick up and k 35 sts along edge of yellow block, join A and pick up and k 35 sts along edge of dark red block, join C and pick up and k 35 sts along edge of dark green block, join E and pick up and k 35 sts along edge of blue block. Work 9 rows in garter st, keeping colors as est

and twisting yarns at color changes. Bind off. Work left edge the same in the foll color sequence: H, D, C, G, F, E, A, B.

Top Fringe Using C and smaller needle, cast on 12 sts.

Rows 1 and 2 Knit.

Row 3 Bind off 10 sts, k to end—2 sts.

Row 4 K2, then cast on 10 sts using the cable cast on—12 sts.

Rows 5 and 6 Knit.

Row 7 As row 3.

Rep rows 4–7 9 more times—11 petals.

Change to H, and rep rows 4–7 9 more times—9 petals.

Change to B, and rep rows 4–7 9 more times—9 petals.

Change to F, and rep rows 4–7 9 more times—9 petals.

Change to D, and rep rows 4–7 9 more times—9 petals.

Change to A, and rep rows 4–7 11 more times—11 petals.

Bind off. Sew fringe to top of afghan.

Work bottom fringe the same in the foll color sequence: C, H, B, F, E, A.

Musical Instruments

This afghan is worked in three stockinette-stitch panels alternating with cabled lace panels. The musical motifs are done in cross-stitch after the stockinette-stitch panels are knit. This technique creates an antique feeling for the piece. The top and bottom eyelet edges are woven with contrasting blue satin ribbon.

KNITTED MEASUREMENTS

52" x 62"/132cm x 157.5cm

MATERIALS

- 11 3½oz/100g skeins (each approx 220yd/201m) of Cascade Yarns *Cascade 220* (100% wool) in #8884 burgundy (A)
- 7 skeins (each approx 8.7yd/8m) of DMC *Tapestry Wool* (100% wool) in #7320 (I)
- 5 skeins each in #7304 (E) and #7473 (M)
- 4 skeins each in #7421 (N) and #7477 (P)
- 3 skeins each in #7386 (H) and #7846 (J)
- 2 skeins each in #7745 (B), #7988 (C), #7544 (D), #7650 (F), #7125 (G), #7919 (K), #7938 (L), #7535 (O), #7078 (Q), #7895 (R), and 7896 (T),
- 1 skein in #7666 (S)
- Size U.S. 8 (5mm) needles OR SIZE TO OBTAIN GAUGE
- Cable needle
- Yarn needle
- 4yd/3.6m Offray Ribbon, single face satin, ¼"/0.5cm wide, in blue

GAUGE

18 sts and 25 rows = 4"/10cm over stockinette st.
TAKE TIME TO CHECK GAUGE.

SPECIAL STITCH

6-st RC—Sl 3 sts to cn and hold to back, k3, k3 from cn.

STOCKINETTE ST PANELS

(make 3)
Using A, cast on 55 sts and work in stockinette st until panel measures 58"/147cm.
Bind off.

LACE CABLE PANELS

(make 4)
Using A, cast on 18 sts.
Row 1 and all odd rows Purl.
Row 2 K1, * yo, ssk, k1, k2tog, yo, k6; rep from * to last 6 sts, yo, ssk, k1, k2tog, yo, k1.
Row 4 K1, * k1, yo, sk2p, yo, k1, 6-st RC; rep from * to last 6 sts, k1, yo, sk2p, yo, k2.
Row 6 As row 2.
Row 8 K1, * k1, yo, sk2p, yo, k8; rep from * to last 5 sts, yo, sk2p, yo, k2.
Rep rows 1–8 until panel measures 58"/147cm.
Bind off.

EMBROIDERY

Work in cross st following charts on stockinette st panels, centering motif on panel.
Stems Using 2 strands of I, work stem st.
Drum zigzag Using 2 strands of D, work chain st.
Violin embellishment Using E, work stem st.
Grape stems Using N, work stem st.

FINISHING

Assembly Sew panels lengthwise, alternating lace cable and stockinette st panels.
Border Cast on 5 sts.
Row 1 (K1, yo) twice, k2tog, kfb.
Row 2 Bind off 2 sts, p to end.
Rep rows 1 and 2 until piece measures 52"/132cm.
Bind off. Sew straight edge to top of afghan. Work bottom edge the same. Thread ribbon through eyelets, secure ends.

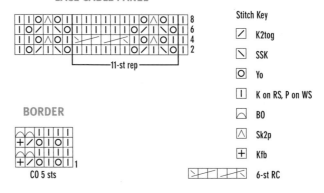

LACE CABLE PANEL

8
6
4
2
—11-st rep—

BORDER

1
CO 5 sts

Stitch Key

⁄	K2tog
＼	SSK
O	Yo
I	K on RS, P on WS
⌒	BO
∧	Sk2p
+	Kfb
	6-st RC

46 *cover up with nicky epstein*

CHART 1

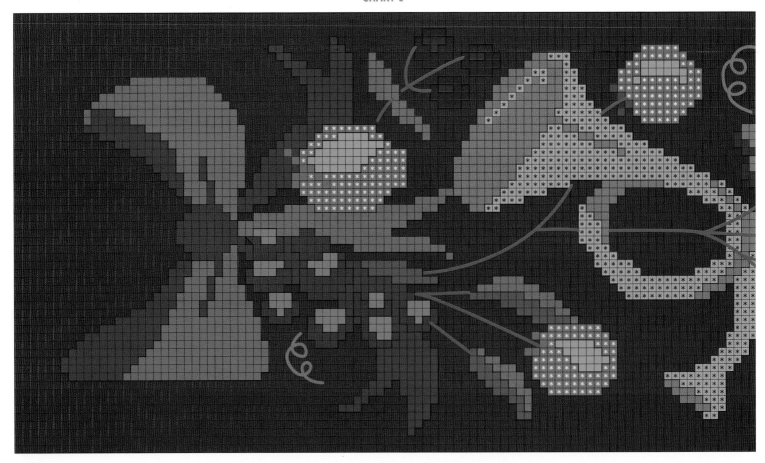

CHART 3

CHART 2

Color Key

- ■ 8884 (A)
- □ 7745 (B)
- ■ 7988 (C)
- ■ 7544 (D)
- ■ 7304 (E)
- ■ 7650 (F)
- ✳ 7125 (G)
- ■ 7386 (H)
- ■ 7320 (I)
- ● 7846 (J)
- ■ 7919 (K)
- ■ 7938 (L)
- ✳ 7473 (M)
- ■ 7421 (N)
- ■ 7535 (O)
- ▬ 7477 (P)
- □ 7078 (Q)
- ■ 7895 (R)
- ■ 7666 (S)
- ■ 7896 (T)

CHART 4

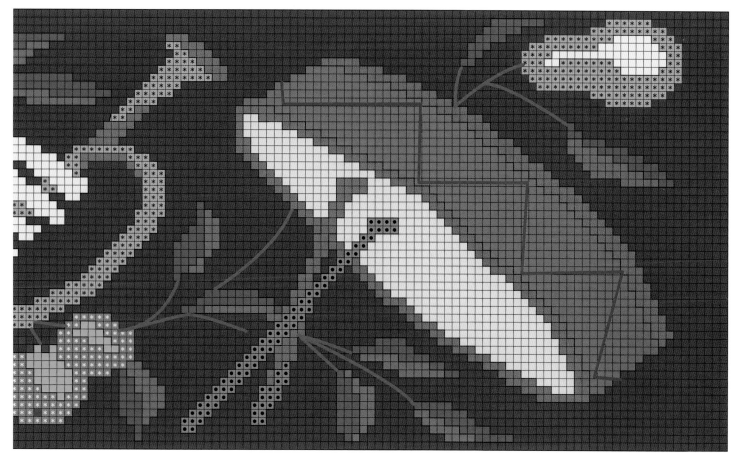

Nature Patchwork

This textural patchwork design has three key techniques, all favorites of mine, that work together to create one unusual piece. Color squares with animal motifs combine with Aran rectangles and smaller squares with grape and leaf appliqués. The border is a mitered garter stitch that I often use on intricate pieces.

KNITTED MEASUREMENTS

44" x 60"/112cm x 152cm

MATERIALS

• 12 4oz/113g skeins (each approx 178 yd/163m) of *Paternayan/ Persian Yarn* (100% wool) from JCA, Inc., in #661 (A)

• 2 skeins of #753 (B)

• 1 skein each in #585 (C), #600 (D), #312 (E), #674 (F), #603 (G), #750 (H), #480 (J), #410 (K), #423 (L), #474 (M), #692 (N), #581 (O), #583 (P), #201 (Q), #203 (R), and #311 (S)

• Size U.S. 7 (4.5mm) needles OR SIZE TO OBTAIN GAUGE

• Size U.S. 7 (4.5mm) circular needle (used as a straight needle), at least 36"/91.5cm OR SIZE TO OBTAIN GAUGE

• Cable needle

• Yarn needle

GAUGE

20 sts and 28 rows = 4"/10cm over stockinette st.
TAKE TIME TO CHECK GAUGE.

SPECIAL STITCHES

LC—Sl 1 st to cn and hold to front, p1, k1 tbl from cn.

RC—Sl 1 st to cn and hold to back, k1 tbl, p1 from cn.

Make bobble—Kfb twice and k1 all into next st—5 sts, turn and purl. Turn and knit, turn and purl, turn and pass 2nd, 3rd, 4th, and 5th sts over 1st—1 st.

REVERSE STOCKINETTE ST

All RS rows Purl.

All WS rows Knit.

ARAN BLOCK

(make 17)

Using A, cast on 47 sts.

Row 1 (RS) * P1, k1 tbl, p3, k1 tbl, p4, k1 tbl, p1, k3 tbl, p1, k1 tbl, p3; rep from * to last 7 sts, p1, k1 tbl, p3, k1 tbl, p1.

Row 2 * K1, p1 tbl, k3, p1 tbl, k4, p1 tbl, k1, p3 tbl, k1, p1 tbl, k3; rep from * to last 7 sts, k1, p1 tbl, k3, p1 tbl, k1.

Row 3 * P1, k1 tbl, p1, make bobble, p1, k1 tbl, p3, RC twice, k1 tbl, LC twice, p2; rep from * to last 7 sts, p1, k1 tbl, p1, make bobble, p1, k1 tbl, p1.

Row 4 * K1, p1 tbl, (k3, p1 tbl) twice, (k1, p1) 4 times, k2; rep from * to last 7 sts, k1, p1 tbl, k3, p1 tbl, k1.

Row 5 * P1, k1 tbl, p3, k1 tbl, p2, RC twice, p1, k1 tbl, p1, LC twice, p1; rep from * to last 7 sts, p1, k1 tbl, p3, k1 tbl, p1.

Row 6 * K1, p1 tbl, k3, p1 tbl, k2, p1 tbl, k1, p1 tbl, (k2, p1 tbl) twice, k1, p1 tbl, k1; rep from * to last 7 sts, k1, p1 tbl, k3, p1 tbl, k1.

Row 7 * P1, k1 tbl, p1, make bobble, p1, k1 tbl, p1, RC twice, p2, k1 tbl, p2, LC twice; rep from * to last 7 sts, p1, k1 tbl, p1, make bobble, p1, k1 tbl, p1.

Row 8 * K1, p1 tbl, k3, p1 tbl, (k1, p1 tbl) twice, (k3, p1 tbl) twice, k1, p1 tbl; rep from * to last 7 sts, k1, p1 tbl, k3, p1 tbl, k1.

Row 9 P1, * k1 tbl, p3, k1 tbl, RC twice, p3, k1 tbl, p3, LC twice; rep from * to last 6 sts, k1 tbl, p3, k1 tbl, p1.

Row 10 K1, * p1 tbl, k3, p2 tbl, k1, p1 tbl, (k4, p1 tbl) twice, k1, p1 tbl; rep from * to last 6 sts, p1 tbl, k3, p1 tbl, k1.

Row 11 P1, * k1 tbl, p1, make bobble, p1, k1 tbl, LC twice, p3, k1 tbl, p3, RC twice; rep from * to last 6 sts, k1 tbl, p1, make bobble, p1, k1 tbl, p1.

Row 12 * K1, p1 tbl, k3, p1 tbl, (k1, p1 tbl) twice, (k3, p1 tbl) twice, k1, p1 tbl; rep from * to last 7 sts, k1, p1 tbl, k3, p1 tbl, k1.

Row 13 * P1, k1 tbl, p3, k1 tbl, p1, LC twice, p2, k1 tbl, p2, RC twice; rep from * to last 7 sts, p1, k1 tbl, p3, k1 tbl, p1.

Row 14 * K1, p1 tbl, k3, p1 tbl, k2, p1 tbl, k1, p1 tbl, (k2, p1 tbl) twice, k1, p1 tbl, k1; rep from * to last 7 sts, k1, p1 tbl, k3, p1 tbl, k1.

Row 15 * P1, k1 tbl, p1, make bobble, p1, k1 tbl, p2, LC twice, p1, k1 tbl, p1, RC twice, p1; rep from * to last 7 sts, p1, k1 tbl, p1, make bobble, p1, k1 tbl, p1.

Row 16 * K1, p1 tbl, (k3, p1 tbl) twice, (k1, p1 tbl) 4 times, k2; rep from * to last 7 sts, k1, p1 tbl, k3, p1 tbl, k1.

Row 17 * P1, k1 tbl, p3, k1 tbl, p3, LC twice, k1 tbl,

RC twice, p2; rep from * to last 7 sts, p1, k1 tbl, p3, k1 tbl, p1.

Row 18 As row 2.

Rep rows 3–18 3 more times.

Bind off.

GRAPE BLOCK

(make 12)

Using B, cast on 37 sts, and work 50 rows in reverse stockinette st.

Bind off.

Leaves (make 24)

Using H, cast on 5 sts.

Row 1 (RS) K2, yo, k1, yo, k2—7 sts.

Row 2 Purl.

Row 3 Using H, k3, yo, k1, yo, using G, k3—9 sts.

Row 4 Using G, p4, using H, p5.

Row 5 Using H, k4, yo, k1, yo, using G, k4—11 sts.

Row 6 Using G, p5, using H, p6.

Row 7 Using H, bind off 3 sts, (k1, yo) twice, using G, k5—10 sts.

Row 8 Using G, bind off 3 sts, p1, using H, p5—7 sts.

Row 9 Using H, k3, (yo, k1) twice, using G, k2—9 sts.

Row 10 Using G, p3, using H, p6.

Row 11 Using H, k4, (yo, k1) twice, using G, k3—11 sts.

Row 12 Using G, p4, using H, p7.

Row 13 Using H, bind off 3 sts, (k1, yo) twice, k1, using G, k4—10 sts.

Row 14 Using G bind off 3 sts, p1, using H, p5—7 sts.

Row 15 Using H, k2tog, k2, using G, k1, k2tog—5 sts.

Row 16 Using G, p3, using H, p2.

Row 17 Using H, k2tog, using G, k1, k2tog—3 sts.

Row 18 Using G, p3.

Row 19 Using G, skp.

Fasten off.

Sew leaves to grape blocks as indicated by chart.

Bobbles (make 144 using E and 144 using S)

Cast on 1 st, make bobble, and fasten off, leaving a long tail.

Sew bobbles to grape blocks as indicated by chart.

EMBROIDERY

Using G, work in stem st for leaf stems.

Using L, work in stem st for grape stems.

Using K, work in stem st for reed stems.

ANIMAL MOTIF BLOCKS

(make 1 for each chart 3–8)

Cast on 49 sts using color indicated by bottom row of each chart, and work chart in stockinette st.

Bind off.

FINISHING

Assembly Sew pieces together as indicated by assembly diagram.

Border Using A and with RS facing, pick up and k 225 sts across top edge.

Row 1 (WS) P1, k to last st, p1.

Row 2 K1, yo, k to last st, yo, k1.

Rep rows 1 and 2 until border measures 1¼"/3cm, then work row 1 once more.

Bind off.

Work bottom edge the same.

Using A and with RS facing, pick up and k 331 sts along one side edge, and work same as top border.

Work other edge the same.

Sew corners together. Weave in all loose ends.

ASSEMBLY DIAGRAM

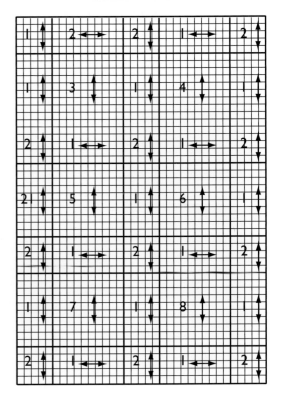

ARAN BLOCK (1)

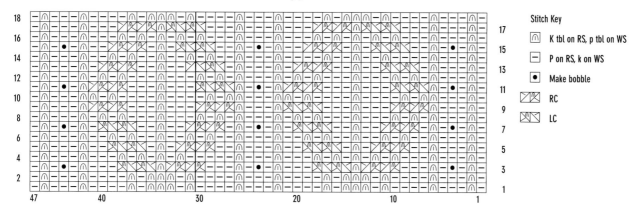

Stitch Key

⌐|⌐ K tbl on RS, p tbl on WS

— P on RS, k on WS

• Make bobble

RC

LC

GRAPE BLOCK DIAGRAM (2)

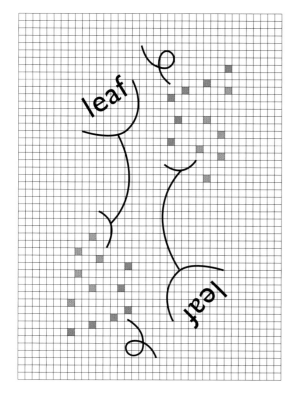

leaf

leaf

OWL (3)

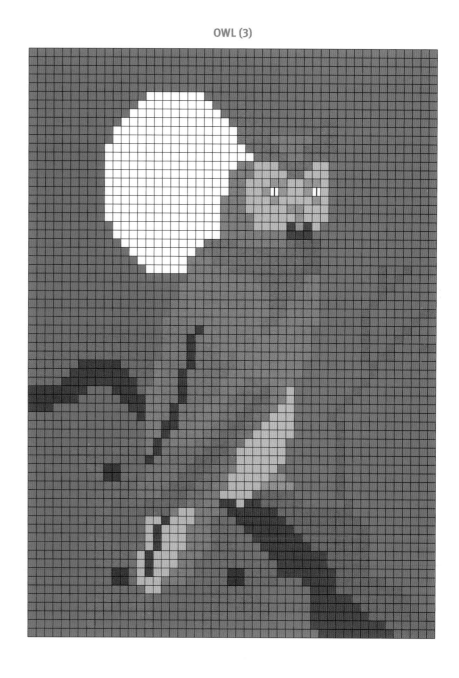

Color Key

753 (B)

674 (F)

750 (H)

410 (K)

423 (L)

474 (M)

692 (N)

581 (O)

201 (Q)

203 (R)

Stitch Key

I Straight Stitch

DEER (4)

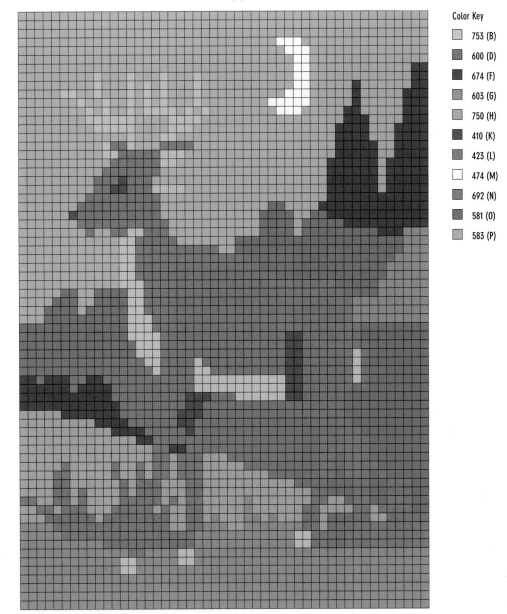

Color Key

- 753 (B)
- 600 (D)
- 674 (F)
- 603 (G)
- 750 (H)
- 410 (K)
- 423 (L)
- 474 (M)
- 692 (N)
- 581 (O)
- 583 (P)

FOX (5)

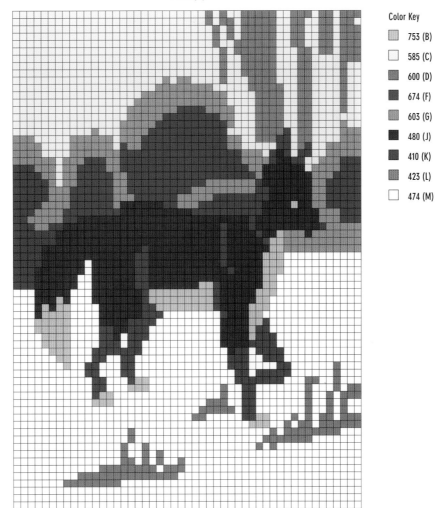

Color Key

- 753 (B)
- 585 (C)
- 600 (D)
- 674 (F)
- 603 (G)
- 480 (J)
- 410 (K)
- 423 (L)
- 474 (M)

DUCK (6)

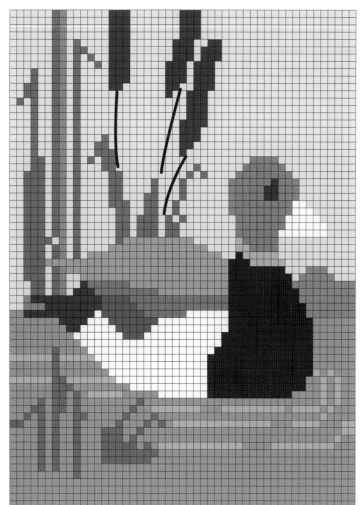

Color Key

- 753 (B)
- 585 (C)
- 600 (D)
- 674 (F)
- 603 (G)
- 750 (H)
- 480 (J)
- 410 (K)
- 423 (L)
- 474 (M)
- 692 (N)
- 581 (O)
- 583 (P)

SQUIRREL (7)

Color Key

- 753 (B)
- 585 (C)
- 674 (F)
- 603 (G)
- 750 (H)
- 410 (K)
- 423 (L)
- 474 (M)
- 201 (Q)
- 203 (R)

RABBIT (8)

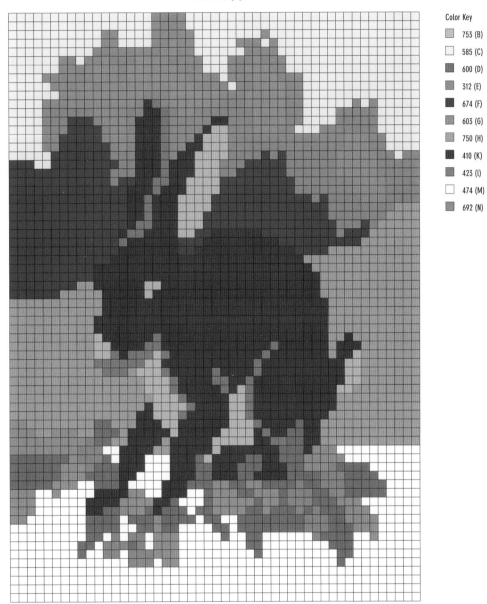

Color Key

- 753 (B)
- 585 (C)
- 600 (D)
- 312 (E)
- 674 (F)
- 603 (G)
- 750 (H)
- 410 (K)
- 423 (l)
- 474 (M)
- 692 (N)

Medieval Tapestry

The center panel of this afghan portrays the same scene twice. Therefore, work the same chart twice: as-is for the first half of the afghan, then upside-down. The sides are worked the same way, as are the top and bottom charts. Note the bobble grapes that are knit into the border, as well as the intarsia bows at each mitered corner, for added interest. The edging is a two-inch folded hem.

KNITTED MEASUREMENTS

46½" x 61½"/118cm x 156cm

MATERIALS

• 12 4oz/113g skeins (each approx 178 yd/163m) of *Paternayan/Persian Yarn* (100% wool) from JCA, Inc., in #920 (I)
• 1 skein each in #530 (A), #910 (B), #924 (C), #840 (D), #870 (E), #967 (F), #830 (G), #832 (H), #406 (J), #471 (K), #435 (L), #730 (M), #741 (N), #320 (O), #734 (P), #605 (Q), #660 (R), #662 (S), #651 (T), #750 (U), #332 (V)
• Size U.S. 7 (4.5mm) needles OR SIZE TO OBTAIN GAUGE
• Yarn bobbins
• Yarn needle

GAUGE

19 sts and 26 rows = 4"/10cm over stockinette st.
TAKE TIME TO CHECK GAUGE.

BOBBLES

Kfb twice and k1 all into next st—5 sts, turn and purl. Turn and knit, turn and purl, turn and pass 2nd, 3rd, 4th, and 5th sts over 1st—1 st. See chart for placement.

CENTER PANEL

Using I, cast on 145 sts. Work in stockinette st foll center panel chart through row 148.
Turn chart upside down, and work it in reverse from row 148 to row 1.
Bind off.

TOP AND BOTTOM BORDERS

Using I, cast on 145 sts.
Row 1 (RS) Work short border chart, then work it again in reverse, being sure to knit center st only once.
Cont as est until short border chart is complete, increasing 1 st at each end of needle every other row 25 times—195 sts.
Purl 1 row on RS for turning ridge.
Using I only, work in stockinette st, and dec 1 st at each end of needle every other row for 1¼"/3cm.
Bind off. Work bottom edge the same.

SIDE BORDERS

Using I, cast on 223 sts.
Row 1 (RS) Work side border chart, then work it again in reverse, being sure to knit center st only once.
Cont as est until side border chart is complete, increasing 1 st at each end of needle every other row 25 times—275 sts.
Work hem same as top and bottom edges.
Work other side edge the same.

EMBROIDERY

Using N, work in stem st for grape tendrils on border.
Using N, S, or T as indicated, work in stem st for stems on main panel.
Using S, work in straight st for leaf veins on main panel.
Using P, work straight st and French knots at center of flowers.
Using E, work straight st for bird's feet.
Using I, work a French knot for bird's eye.
Using K, work a French knot for rabbit's eye.

FINISHING

Assembly Sew border pieces to center panel. Sew corners together. Fold hems to WS and sew down. Weave in all loose ends.

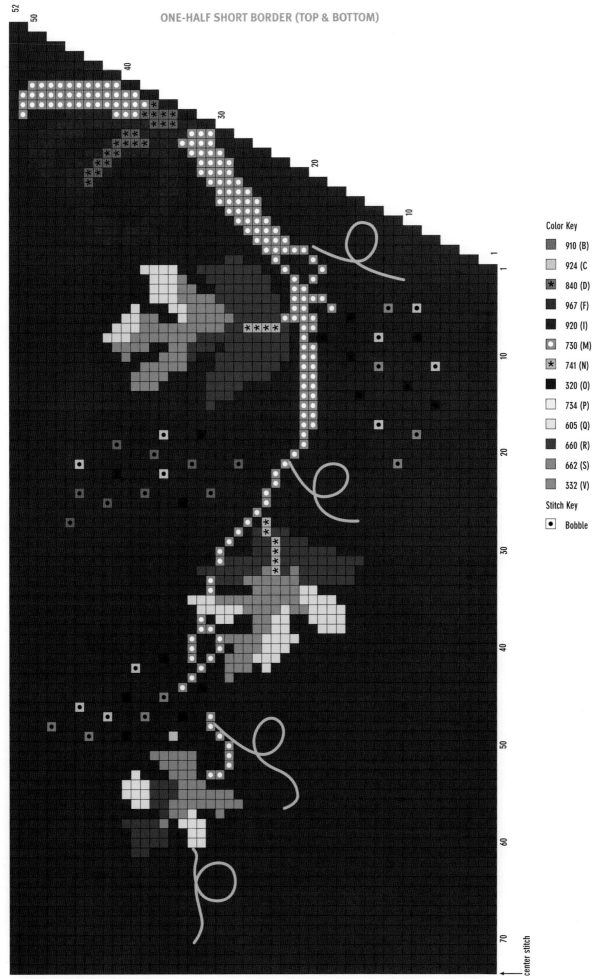

Color Key

- ■ 910 (B)
- ▨ 924 (C
- ✳ 840 (D)
- ■ 967 (F)
- ■ 920 (I)
- ◉ 730 (M)
- ✳ 741 (N)
- ■ 320 (O)
- □ 734 (P)
- ▨ 605 (Q)
- ■ 660 (R)
- ▨ 662 (S)
- ▨ 332 (V)

Stitch Key

- ◉ Bobble

center stitch

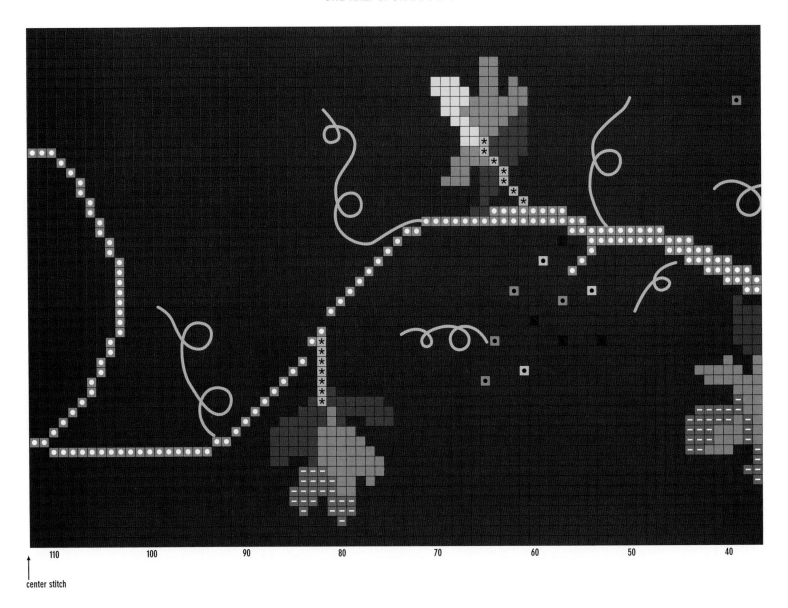

110   100   90   80   70   60   50   40

center stitch

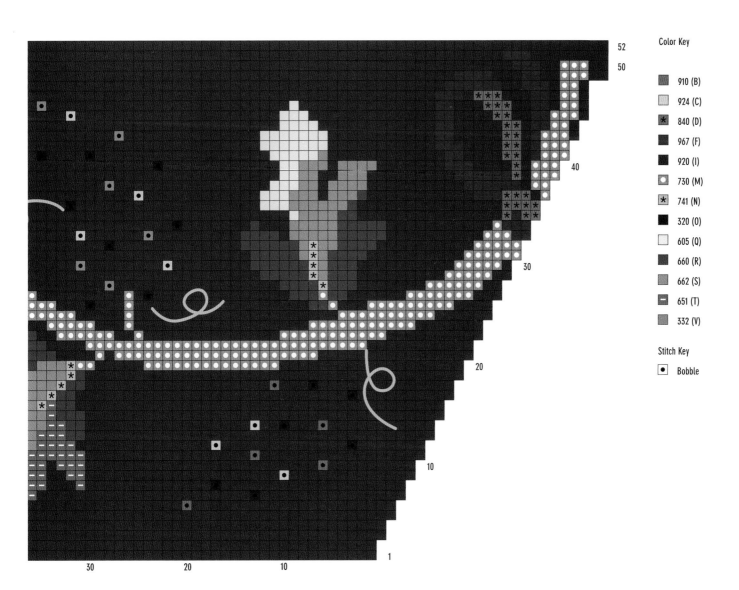

Color Key

- 910 (B)
- 924 (C)
- ✳ 840 (D)
- 967 (F)
- 920 (I)
- ◉ 730 (M)
- ✳ 741 (N)
- 320 (O)
- 605 (Q)
- 660 (R)
- 662 (S)
- − 651 (T)
- 332 (V)

Stitch Key

- ● Bobble

145

Color Key

910 (B)		832 (H)	✳	741 (N)	—	651 (T)	
840 (D)		920 (I)		734 (P)	—	750 (U)	
V 870 (E)		471 (K)		605 (Q)			
967 (F)		435 (L)		660 (R)			
830 (G)		730 (M)		662 (S)			

cover up with nicky epstein

70

60

50

40

30

20

10

1

1

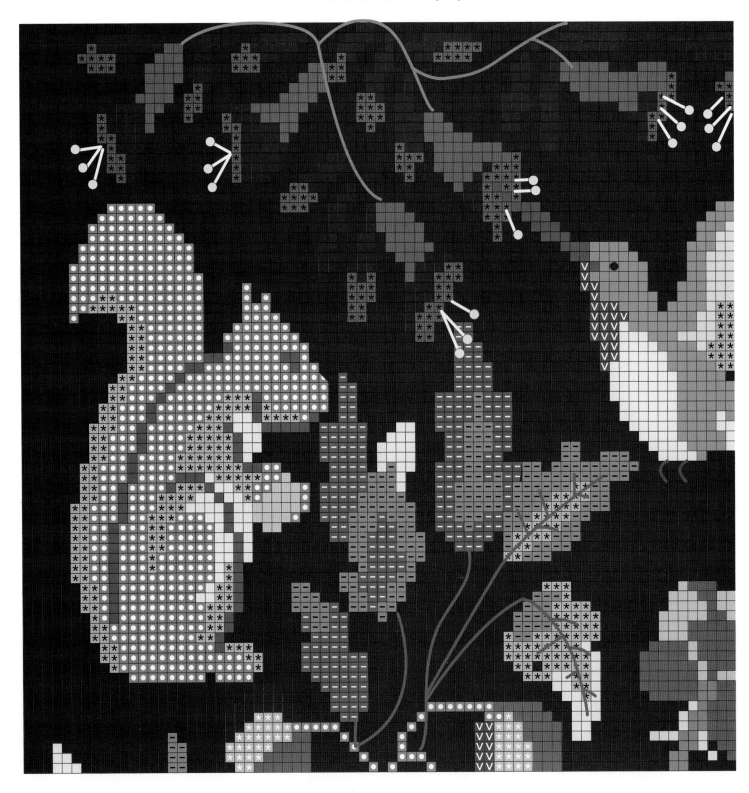

Color Key

530 (A)	830 (G)	435 (L)	605 (Q)				
910 (B)	832 (H)	730 (M)	660 (R)				
924 (C)	920 (I)	741 (N)	662 (S)				
840 (D)	406 (J)	320 (O)	651 (T)				
870 (E)	471 (K)	734 (P)	750 (U)				
967 (F)							

Stitch Key

◎ French Knot

148

140

130

120

110

100

90

80

Twelve Days of Christmas

This was one of my first Christmas afghans, inspired by my favorite Christmas carol.

The background is knit in intarsia using a DK yarn and some metallic, with

embroidery stitches for the detail in each panel. I chose colors that would depict the

feel of a castle or elegant manor rather than the traditional Christmas colors. Not

using Christmas colors was a gamble, but it worked.

KNITTED MEASUREMENTS
42" x 71"/106.5cm x 117.5cm

MATERIALS
• 5 (1¾oz/50g) skeins (each approx 137 yd/125m) RYC/Westminster Fibers, Inc., *Pure Wool DK* (100% superwash wool) in #028 Raspberry (A), and #032 Gilt (B)
• 4 skeins each in #019 Avocado (C), and #014 Hay (D)
• 3 skeins each in #020 Parsley (E), #007 Cypress (F), #006 Pier (G), #017 Mocha (L), #008 Marine (P), and #021 Glade (S)
• 2 skeins each in #023 Shamrock (H), #029 Pomegranate (I), #037 Port (J), #004 Black (K), #015 Barley (M), #039 Lavender (N), #030 Damson (O), #016 Hessian (Q), #013 Enamel (R), #036 Kiss (T), #035 Quarry (U), and #003 Anthracite (V)
• 2 (1¾ oz/50g) skeins (each approx 123 yd/130 m) of Rowan/Westminster Fibers, Inc., *Scottish Tweed DK* (100% wool) in #017 Lobster
• Gold metallic yarn
• Size U.S. 7 (4.5mm) circular needle (used as a straight needle), at least 36"/91.5cm length OR SIZE TO OBTAIN GAUGE
• Size H/8 (5mm) crochet hook
• Yarn needle
• Fabric for backing (optional)

GAUGE
20 sts and 26 rows = 4"/10cm over stockinette st.
TAKE TIME TO CHECK GAUGE.

NOTE
Background sections 1–4 are knitted in order in one piece from the bottom up. Be sure to use the appropriate color key for each section. Background of afghan is knit working charts 1 and 2. The 12-days motifs are worked in duplicate st after piece is completed.

SECTION 1
Using O, cast on 212 sts. Knit 4 rows for hem.
Next row (RS) K2 (selvage), * work 8 sts of chart 1; rep from * to last 2 sts, k2 (selvage).
Cont as est until chart 1 is complete.
Next row K2 (selvage), * work 69 sts of chart 2; rep from * to last 3 sts, work 1st st of chart 2 again, k2 (selvage).
Cont as est until chart 2 is complete.

SECTION 2
Work same as section 1, except in 3rd rep of chart 2 (at left side of afghan), eliminate checkerboard pattern, and work that area using G only (omitting Q).

SECTION 3
Work same as section 1.

SECTION 4
Work same as section 1. After completing chart 2, work 11 rows of chart 1, working small dot on chart with D. Work 2 rows D, then work rows 1–4 of chart 1, working small dot with G. With O, k 4 rows for facing. Bind off.

EMBROIDERY
Work rem charts in duplicate st, aligning center square of each chart (as indicated by ■)with center square of chart 2, in the foll order (left to right, top to bottom): partridge, doves, hens, calling birds, gold rings, goose, swan, maid, drummer, piper, lady, lord.
Doves: Using T, work 3 French knots for mistletoe. Using E, work 2 French knots for eyes. Using B, work straight st for feet.
Lady: Using F, work lazy daisy sts for flowers on skirt. Using B, work French knots at center of flowers. Using T, work straight st for mouth. Using F, work straight st for eye.
Lord: Using H, work straight st for pants cuffs. Using T, work straight st for mouth and buttons. Using F, work straight st for eye.
Piper: Using H, work stem st for banner straps. Using I, work stem st for hat band. Using K, work straight st for eye.
Drummer: Using B, work stem st for drum definition. Using Q, work stem st for drumsticks. Using T, work straight st for mouth and jacket detail. Using L, work straight st for eye.

FINISHING
Assembly: Fold hems to WS and sew down.
Weave in all loose ends.
Sew backing fabric if desired.
Border: Using O, work 1 row in sc around afghan, working 3 sc into each corner. Fasten off.

CHART 2

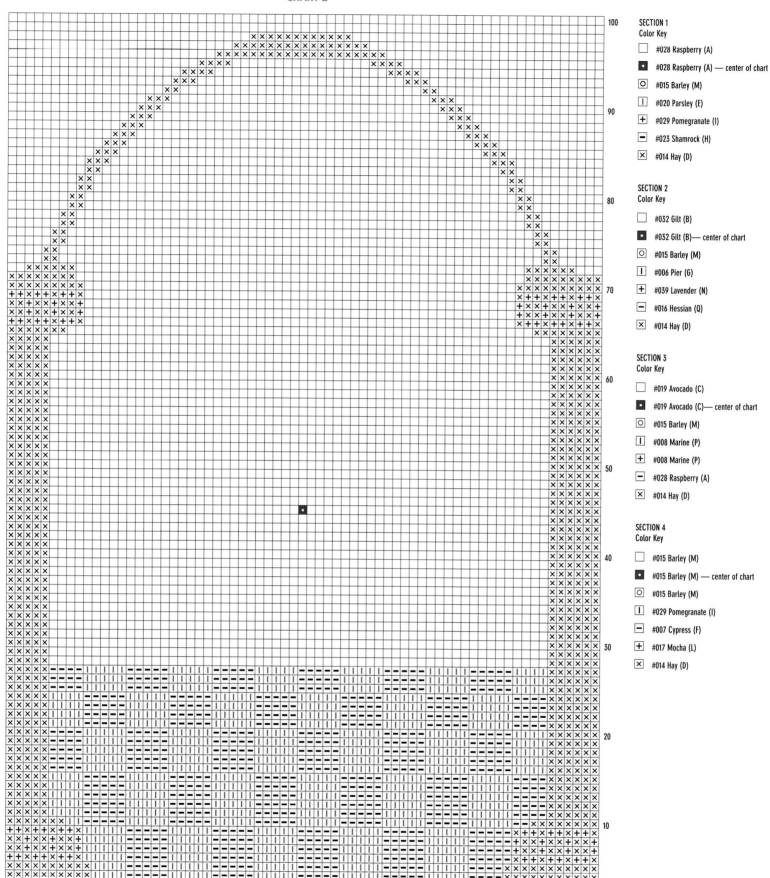

SECTION 1
Color Key

☐ #028 Raspberry (A)

▣ #028 Raspberry (A) — center of chart

⊡ #015 Barley (M)

Ⅰ #020 Parsley (E)

⊞ #029 Pomegranate (I)

⊟ #023 Shamrock (H)

☒ #014 Hay (D)

SECTION 2
Color Key

☐ #032 Gilt (B)

▣ #032 Gilt (B) — center of chart

⊡ #015 Barley (M)

Ⅰ #006 Pier (G)

⊞ #039 Lavender (N)

⊟ #016 Hessian (Q)

☒ #014 Hay (D)

SECTION 3
Color Key

☐ #019 Avocado (C)

▣ #019 Avocado (C) — center of chart

⊡ #015 Barley (M)

Ⅰ #008 Marine (P)

⊞ #008 Marine (P)

⊟ #028 Raspberry (A)

☒ #014 Hay (D)

SECTION 4
Color Key

☐ #015 Barley (M)

▣ #015 Barley (M) — center of chart

⊡ #015 Barley (M)

Ⅰ #029 Pomegranate (I)

⊟ #007 Cypress (F)

⊞ #017 Mocha (L)

☒ #014 Hay (D)

69 sts

CHART 1

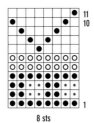

8 sts

Color Key

☐ #039 Lavendar (N)

◯ #015 Barley (M)

● #030 Damson (O)

⊡ Section 1 #039 Lavendar (N)

Section 2: #028 Raspberry (A)

Section 3: #032 Gilt (B)

Section 4: #019 Avocado (C)

PARTRIDGE

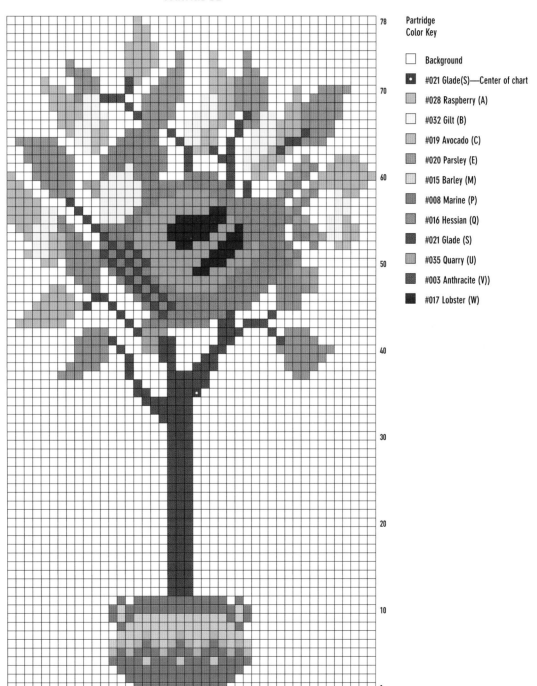

44 sts

Partridge Color Key

☐ Background

▪ #021 Glade(S)—Center of chart

▨ #028 Raspberry (A)

☐ #032 Gilt (B)

▨ #019 Avocado (C)

▨ #020 Parsley (E)

▨ #015 Barley (M)

▨ #008 Marine (P)

▨ #016 Hessian (Q)

▨ #021 Glade (S)

▨ #035 Quarry (U)

▨ #003 Anthracite (V))

▪ #017 Lobster (W)

DOVES

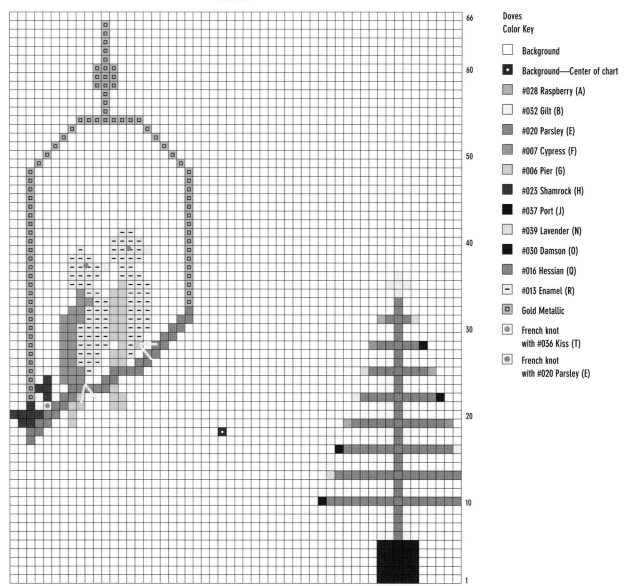

Doves
Color Key

☐ Background

▣ Background—Center of chart

▨ #028 Raspberry (A)

☐ #032 Gilt (B)

▨ #020 Parsley (E)

▨ #007 Cypress (F)

▨ #006 Pier (G)

■ #023 Shamrock (H)

■ #037 Port (J)

▨ #039 Lavender (N)

■ #030 Damson (O)

▨ #016 Hessian (Q)

– #013 Enamel (R)

▢ Gold Metallic

● French knot
with #036 Kiss (T)

◉ French knot
with #020 Parsley (E)

54 sts

HENS

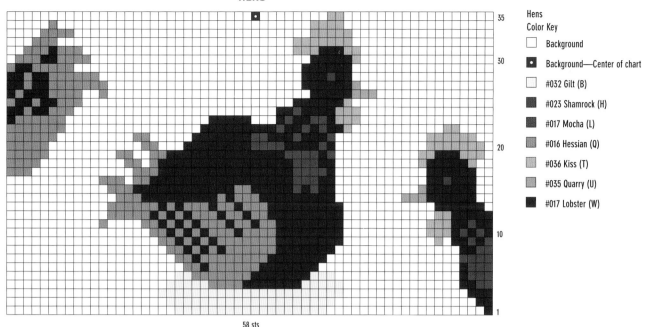

35
30
20
10
1

58 sts

**Hens
Color Key**

☐ Background

⊡ Background—Center of chart

☐ #032 Gilt (B)

■ #023 Shamrock (H)

■ #017 Mocha (L)

■ #016 Hessian (Q)

■ #036 Kiss (T)

■ #035 Quarry (U)

■ #017 Lobster (W)

CALLING BIRDS

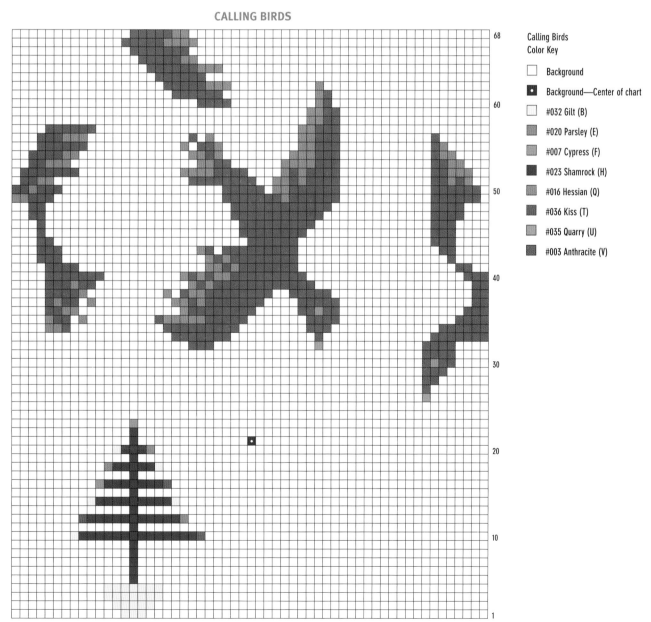

68
60
50
40
30
20
10
1

57 sts

**Calling Birds
Color Key**

☐ Background

⊡ Background—Center of chart

☐ #032 Gilt (B)

■ #020 Parsley (E)

■ #007 Cypress (F)

■ #023 Shamrock (H)

■ #016 Hessian (Q)

■ #036 Kiss (T)

■ #035 Quarry (U)

■ #003 Anthracite (V)

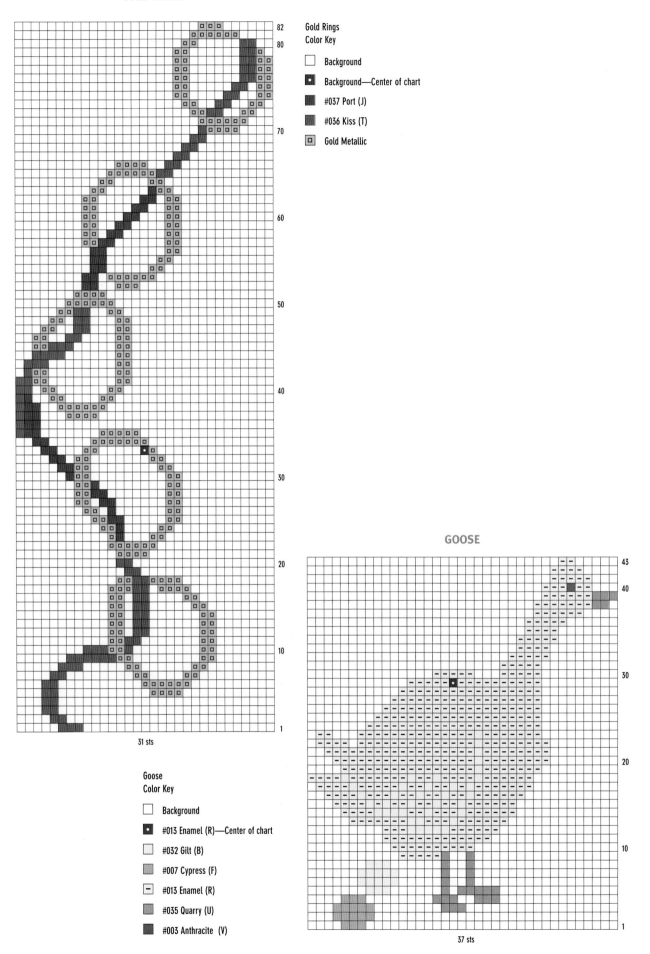

GOLD RINGS

Gold Rings
Color Key

☐ Background

◼ Background—Center of chart

◼ #037 Port (J)

◼ #036 Kiss (T)

▣ Gold Metallic

31 sts

GOOSE

Goose
Color Key

☐ Background

◼ #013 Enamel (R)—Center of chart

☐ #032 Gilt (B)

▨ #007 Cypress (F)

− #013 Enamel (R)

▨ #035 Quarry (U)

◼ #003 Anthracite (V)

37 sts

SWAN

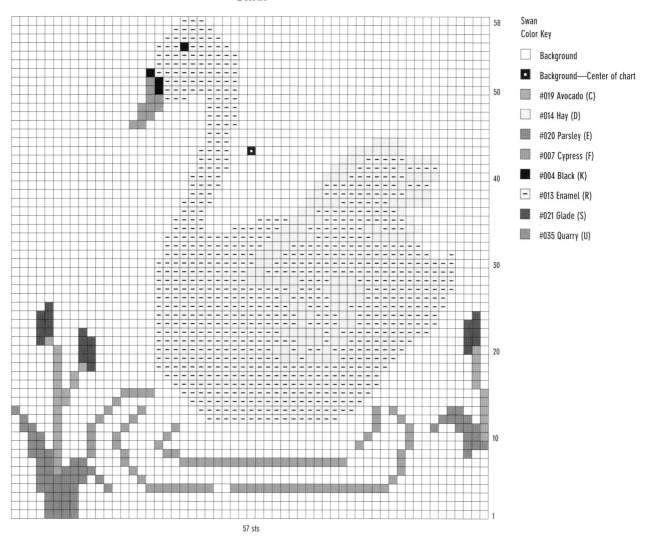

Swan Color Key

- ☐ Background
- ⊡ Background—Center of chart
- ▨ #019 Avocado (C)
- ☐ #014 Hay (D)
- ▨ #020 Parsley (E)
- ▨ #007 Cypress (F)
- ■ #004 Black (K)
- − #013 Enamel (R)
- ▨ #021 Glade (S)
- ▨ #035 Quarry (U)

57 sts

MAID

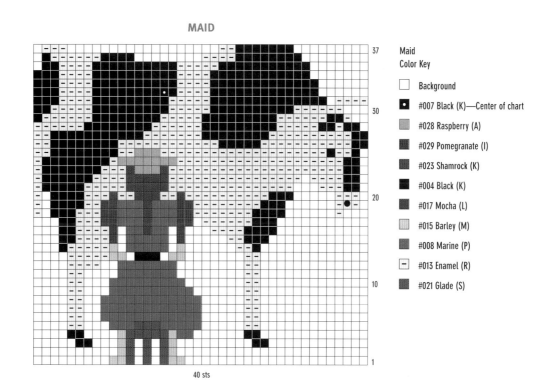

Maid Color Key

- ☐ Background
- ⊡ #007 Black (K)—Center of chart
- ▨ #028 Raspberry (A)
- ▨ #029 Pomegranate (I)
- ▨ #023 Shamrock (K)
- ■ #004 Black (K)
- ▨ #017 Mocha (L)
- ☐ #015 Barley (M)
- ▨ #008 Marine (P)
- − #013 Enamel (R)
- ▨ #021 Glade (S)

40 sts

DRUMMER

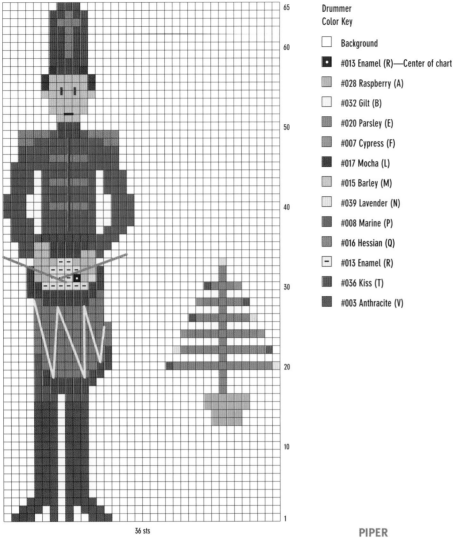

65

60

50

40

30

20

10

1

36 sts

Drummer
Color Key

☐ Background

◼ #013 Enamel (R)—Center of chart

☐ #028 Raspberry (A)

☐ #032 Gilt (B)

☐ #020 Parsley (E)

☐ #007 Cypress (F)

◼ #017 Mocha (L)

☐ #015 Barley (M)

☐ #039 Lavender (N)

☐ #008 Marine (P)

☐ #016 Hessian (Q)

− #013 Enamel (R)

☐ #036 Kiss (T)

◼ #003 Anthracite (V)

PIPER

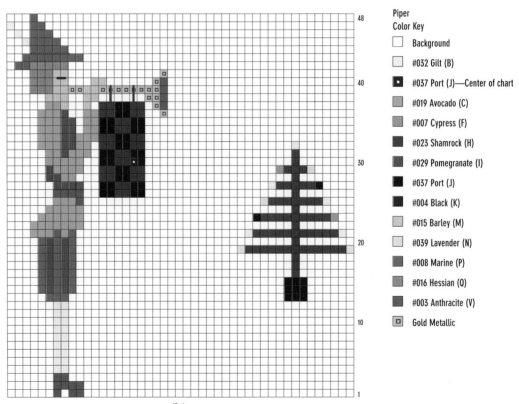

48

40

30

20

10

1

45 sts

Piper
Color Key

☐ Background

☐ #032 Gilt (B)

◼ #037 Port (J)—Center of chart

☐ #019 Avocado (C)

☐ #007 Cypress (F)

◼ #023 Shamrock (H)

☐ #029 Pomegranate (I)

◼ #037 Port (J)

◼ #004 Black (K)

☐ #015 Barley (M)

☐ #039 Lavender (N)

☐ #008 Marine (P)

☐ #016 Hessian (Q)

☐ #003 Anthracite (V)

☐ Gold Metallic

LADY

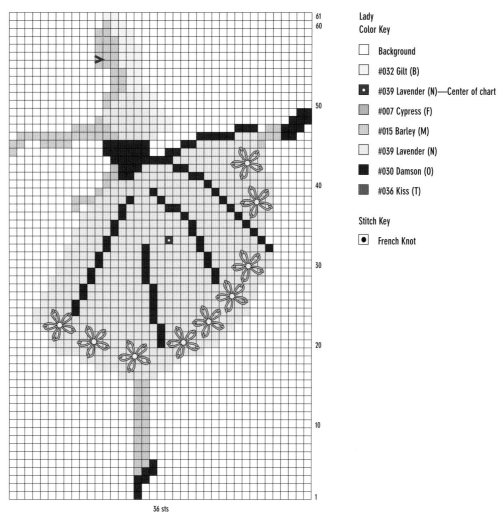

61
60

50

40

30

20

10

1

36 sts

**Lady
Color Key**

☐ Background

☐ #032 Gilt (B)

■ #039 Lavender (N)—Center of chart

▨ #007 Cypress (F)

▨ #015 Barley (M)

☐ #039 Lavender (N)

■ #030 Damson (O)

▨ #036 Kiss (T)

Stitch Key

⦿ French Knot

LORD

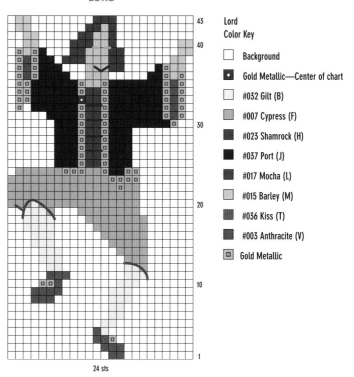

43
40

30

20

10

1

24 sts

**Lord
Color Key**

☐ Background

▣ Gold Metallic—Center of chart

☐ #032 Gilt (B)

▨ #007 Cypress (F)

■ #023 Shamrock (H)

■ #037 Port (J)

■ #017 Mocha (L)

▨ #015 Barley (M)

▨ #036 Kiss (T)

■ #003 Anthracite (V)

▣ Gold Metallic

cover up with nicky epstein

Twelve Months

This afghan and the zodiac design in this book were originally published in a
magazine that spread out the instructions over four issues. To this day, I receive
many requests for the full instructions from knitters who missed one or two issues,
and I am happy to publish them here in full for the first time. The Twelve Months
motif was inspired by an antique silver bracelet that I purchased at a flea market in
Paris. I still love the bracelet. The afghan blocks are intarsia with some embroidery,
and they are framed with I-cord and then sewn together. I also sewed stockinette
I-cord around the edge to finish off the whole piece.

Each square 13" x 15"/33cm x 38cm not including cord edging
Afghan 42" x 62"/106.5cm x 156.5cm

MATERIALS

• 5 4oz/113g skeins (each approx 178 yd/163m) of *Paternayan Persian Yarn* from JCA, Inc., (100% wool) each in #530 (A) and #660 (D)
• 1 skein each in #941 (B) #633 (C), #513 (E), #507 (F), #652 (G), #853 (H), #310 (I), #480 (J), #703 (K), #262 (L), #679 (M), #707 (N), #571 (O), #967 (P), #654 (Q), #604 (R), #333 (S), #321 (T), #924 (U), #421 (V), #462 (W), #416 (X), #770 (Y), #553 (Z), #912 (BB), #330 (CC), #602 (DD), #442 (EE)
• 1 skein of gold metallic
• Size U.S. 7 (4.5mm) needles OR SIZE TO OBTAIN GAUGE
• Set of double pointed needles in same size (for I-cords)
• Yarn needle

GAUGE

20 sts and 26 rows = 4"/10cm over stockinette st.
TAKE TIME TO CHECK GAUGE.

SEED ST

(odd number of sts)
Every row K1, * p1, k1; rep from * to end.

SQUARES

(make 1 for each month chart)
Using A, cast on 63 sts, and work in seed st for 1¼"/3cm.
Next row RS Using A, work 7 sts in seed st, then work 49 sts of chart in stockinette st, then work 7 sts in seed st using A again.
Continue in this manner until chart is complete.
Using A, work in seed st for 1¼"/3cm.
Bind off in pattern.
Using D, create a 64"/162.5cm I-cord, and sew around border of square.

EMBROIDERY

January Using V, work straight st for fence. Using B, work straight st for birds.
February Using Y, C, and BB, work stem st for balloon strings.
March Using G, work straight st for stems and leaves. Using S and CC, work straight st for flower petals. Using K, work straight st at center of flowers.
April Using V, work stem st for cherry stems.
May Using C, work straight st for leaf veins.
June Using V, work stem st across bucket. Using A, work lazy daisy sts for bee wings.
July Using Y, work French knots at center of flowers.
August Using V, work stem st for birds.
September Using V, work stem st for grape stems.
October Using J, work stem st to section pumpkin. Using V, work stem st for cherry stem, and straight st for pear, apple and banana stems. Using I, work French knots for flowers. Using G, work stem st for pumpkin stem. Using X, work straight st for flower stems.
November Using DD, work stem st for leaf veins and flower definitions.
December Using gold metallic, work chain st across tree, and straight st to create star at top. Using B and C, work French knots for ornaments.

FINISHING

Assembly Using D, sew squares together.
Border Using D, create a 212"/538cm I-cord, and sew around border of afghan.

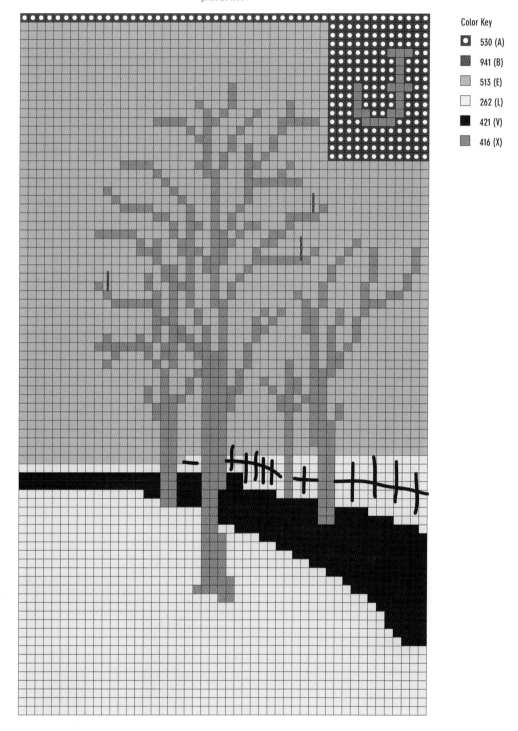

Color Key

- ⊙ 530 (A)
- ▨ 941 (B)
- ▨ 513 (E)
- ☐ 262 (L)
- ■ 421 (V)
- ▨ 416 (X)

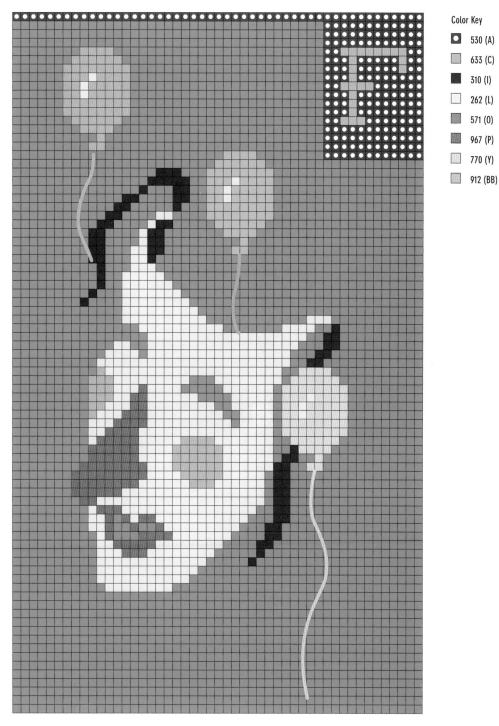

Color Key

- 530 (A)
- 633 (C)
- 310 (I)
- 262 (L)
- 571 (O)
- 967 (P)
- 770 (Y)
- 912 (BB)

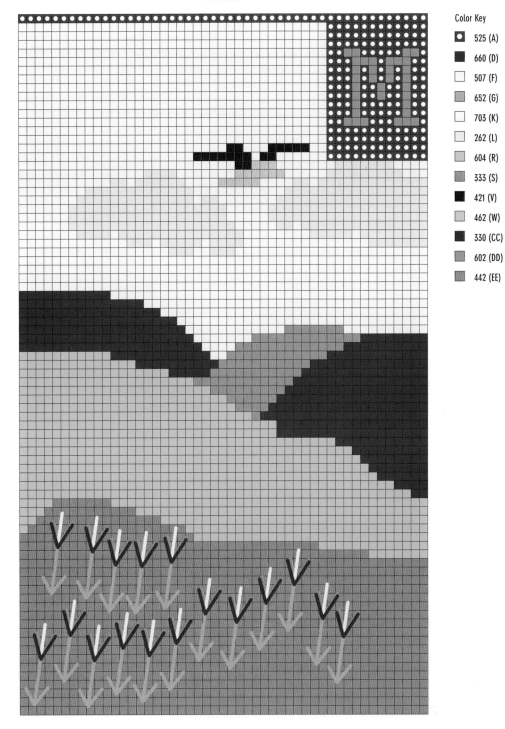

Color Key

⬡ 525 (A)
⬛ 660 (D)
⬜ 507 (F)
▨ 652 (G)
☐ 703 (K)
▢ 262 (L)
▨ 604 (R)
▨ 333 (S)
⬛ 421 (V)
▨ 462 (W)
⬛ 330 (CC)
▨ 602 (DD)
▨ 442 (EE)

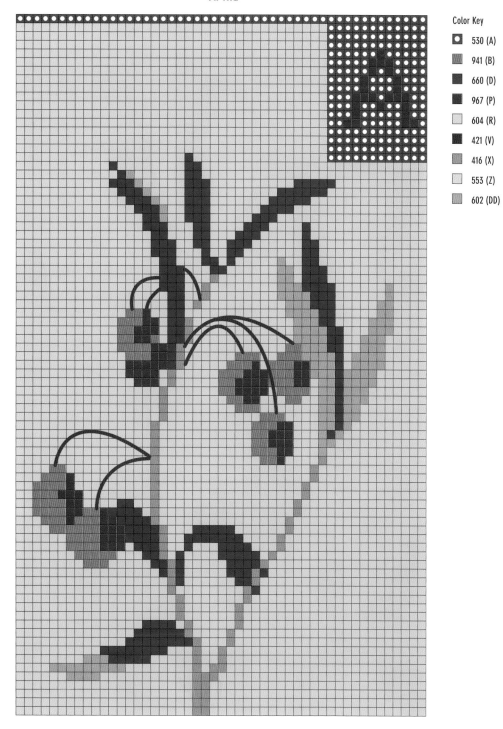

Color Key

 530 (A)

941 (B)

660 (D)

967 (P)

604 (R)

421 (V)

416 (X)

553 (Z)

602 (DD)

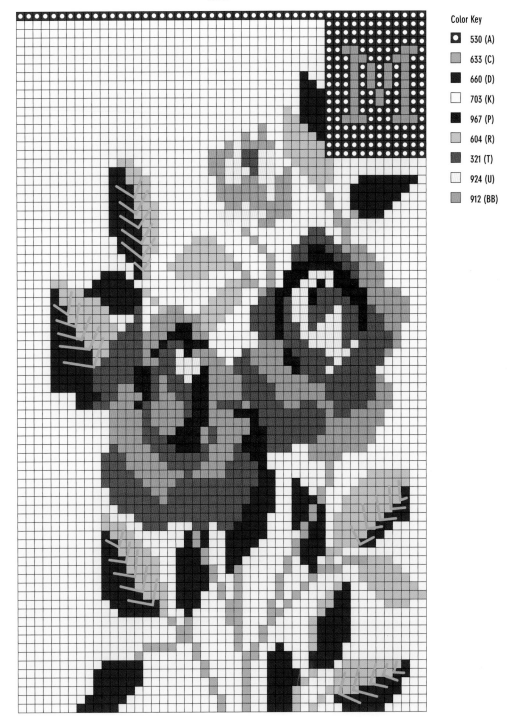

Color Key

- 530 (A)
- 633 (C)
- 660 (D)
- 703 (K)
- 967 (P)
- 604 (R)
- 321 (T)
- 924 (U)
- 912 (BB)

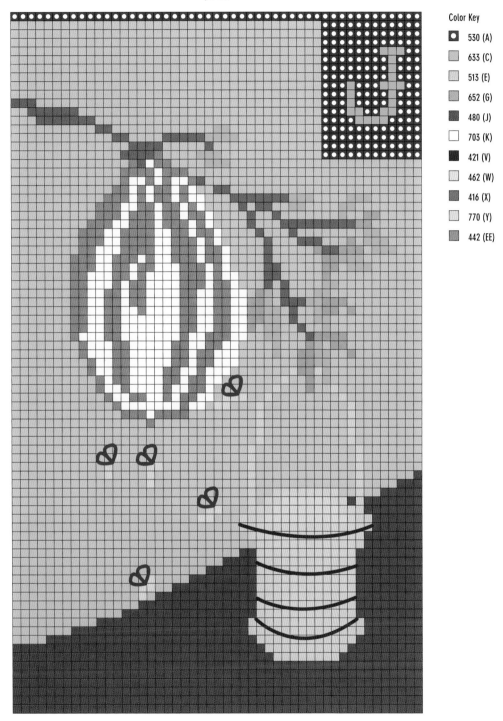

Color Key

- 530 (A)
- 633 (C)
- 513 (E)
- 652 (G)
- 480 (J)
- 703 (K)
- 421 (V)
- 462 (W)
- 416 (X)
- 770 (Y)
- 442 (EE)

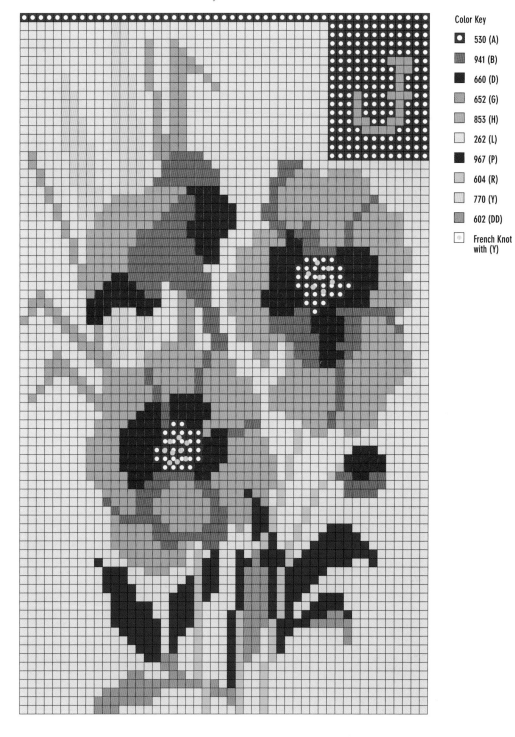

Color Key

- 530 (A)
- 941 (B)
- 660 (D)
- 652 (G)
- 853 (H)
- 262 (L)
- 967 (P)
- 604 (R)
- 770 (Y)
- 602 (DD)
- French Knot with (Y)

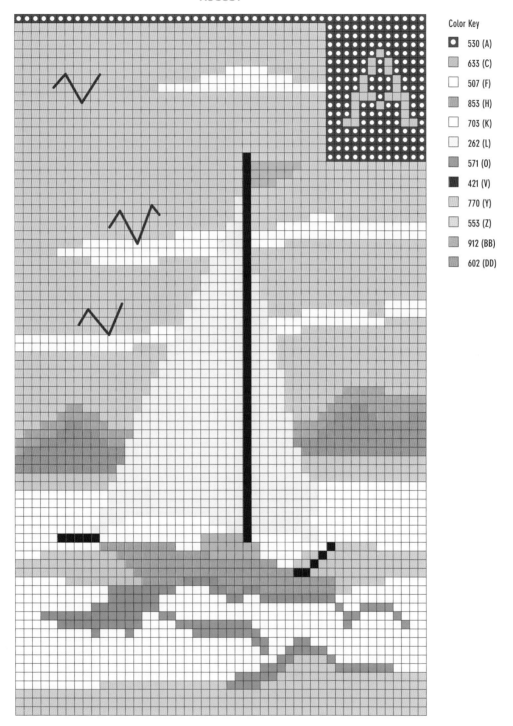

Color Key

- ⬤ 530 (A)
- ⬜ 633 (C)
- ⬜ 507 (F)
- ⬜ 853 (H)
- ⬜ 703 (K)
- ⬜ 262 (L)
- ⬜ 571 (O)
- ▨ 421 (V)
- ⬜ 770 (Y)
- ⬜ 553 (Z)
- ⬜ 912 (BB)
- ⬜ 602 (DD)

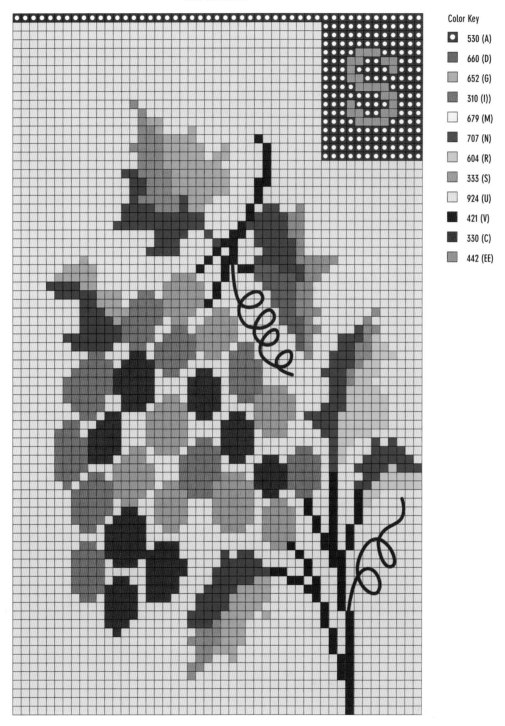

Color Key

- ⬭ 530 (A)
- ⬛ 660 (D)
- ⬛ 652 (G)
- ⬛ 310 (I))
- ⬜ 679 (M)
- ⬛ 707 (N)
- ⬛ 604 (R)
- ⬛ 333 (S)
- ⬜ 924 (U)
- ⬛ 421 (V)
- ⬛ 330 (C)
- ⬛ 442 (EE)

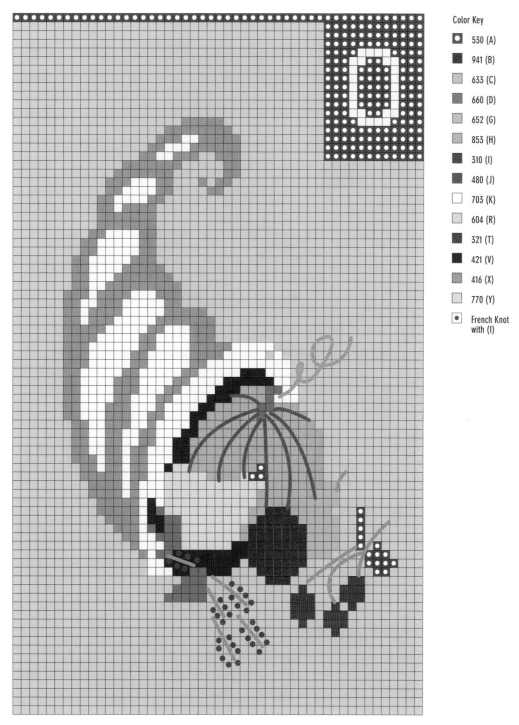

Color Key

⬤	530 (A)
⬛	941 (B)
⬜	633 (C)
⬛	660 (D)
⬜	652 (G)
⬜	853 (H)
⬛	310 (I)
⬛	480 (J)
⬜	703 (K)
⬜	604 (R)
⬛	321 (T)
⬛	421 (V)
⬜	416 (X)
⬜	770 (Y)
⊡	French Knot with (I)

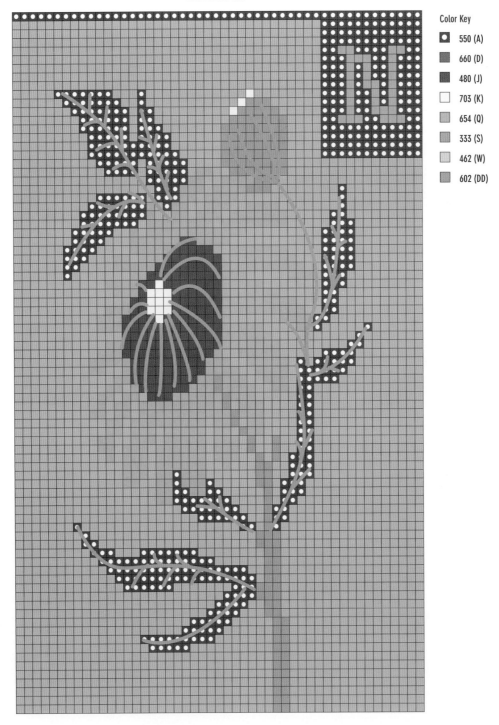

Color Key

- 550 (A)
- 660 (D)
- 480 (J)
- 703 (K)
- 654 (Q)
- 333 (S)
- 462 (W)
- 602 (DD)

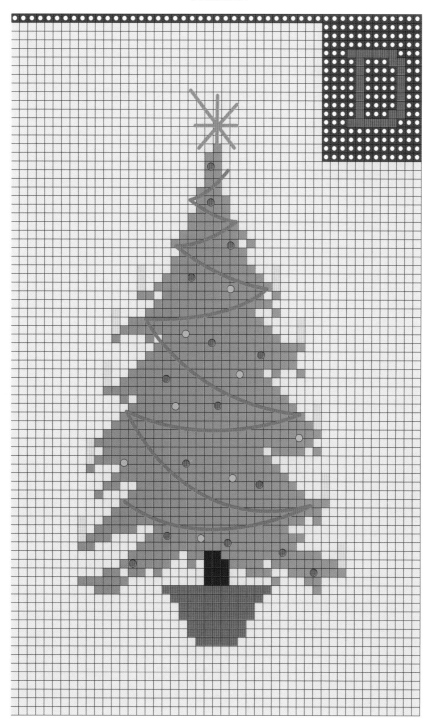

Color Key

◉	531 (A)
▦	941 (B)
▨	633 (C)
▢	262 (L)
▨	707 (N)
■	421 (V)
▨	770 (Y)
▨	Gold Metallic (FF)
◉	French Knot

Zodiac

For all of you who have requested this pattern over the years . . . here it is. Sorry it took so long. Tip: If you don't want to make the whole afghan, choose your favorite zodiacal sign and make a bag or pillow. The zodiac motifs are knit in a combination of intarsia, stitch patterns, appliqué and embroidery. The blocks are connected by knit cord, and, at each inside corner, by embroidered floral accents.

Each square 16" x 16"/41cm x 41cm
Afghan 52" x 68"/132cm x 173cm

MATERIALS

• 8 3.5oz/100g skeins (each approx 220yd/242m) of Cascade Yarns *Cascade 220* (100% Peruvian Highland wool) in #8383 navy (A)
• 2 skeins in #2411 dark rust (B)
• 1 skein each in #8339 dusty blue (C), #7815 light blue (D), #9473 grey (E), #8021 flesh (F), #2415 gold (G), #8555 black (H), #9471 brown (I), #8010 ecru (J), #7821 taupe (K), #9427 teal (L), #8884 scarlet (M) and #2414 rust (N)
• 1 skein each of gold metallic, silver metallic, bronze metallic, and white metallic yarn
• Size U.S. 7 (4.5mm) circular needle (used as a straight needle), 24/61cm" length OR SIZE TO OBTAIN GAUGE
• Set of double pointed needles in same size (for I-cords)
• Size F/7 (4.5mm) crochet hook, or size to correspond with knitting needles
• Yarn needle

GAUGE

20 sts and 28 rows = 4"/10cm over stockinette st.
TAKE TIME TO CHECK GAUGE.

SQUARES

(make 1 for each chart)

Using A, cast on 79 sts. Work chart, then bind off.

Using A, work 1 row in sc around square, working 3 sc into each corner. Fasten off.

I-CORDS

Using G, create a 5-st I-cord 12"/30cm long for Leo's tail.

Using 1 strand of L and 1 strand of gold metallic, create a 6-st I-cord 27"/69cm long for Libra's serpent.

Using E, create a 3-st I-cord 10"/25cm long for Taurus' tail.

EMBROIDERY

Aries Using H, work straight st and French knots for face definition. Using bronze metallic, work in stem st on horns.

Taurus Sew down I-cord for tail. Using 2 strands of E held together, work in stem st for tip of tail and brow. Using white metallic, work straight st and French knots for breath.

Gemini Using C, work straight st for eyes. Using O, work straight st for mouths. Using gold metallic, work double cross st for stars.

Leo Sew down I-cord for tail. Using bronze metallic, work in duplicate st on mane and tip of tail.

Virgo Using gold metallic, work in stem st for wing definition. Using K, work in stem st for body definition. Using L, work in stem st for flower stems and lazy daisy st for leaves. Using M, work straight st for mouth and French knots for flower centers. Using C, work straight st for eyes.

Libra Sew down I-cord for serpent. Using gold metallic, create 3 crochet chains 8"/20cm long, and sew down at ends for scale chains. Using O,

work straight st for serpent's mouth and eyes.

Scorpio Using silver metallic, work double cross st for stars, stem st for outlines, and straight st for claws.

Sagittarius Work in stem st using J for bow, L for arrow, and I for body definition. Using gold metallic, work straight st for wrist guards and arrow's point.

Capricorn Using silver metallic, work trellis st on tail as indicated by chart.

Pisces Using bronze metallic, work in trellis st for scales and stem st for tail definition.

FINISHING

Assembly Using B, join squares by working in scs. Using B, embroider a flower in corner where squares are joined.

Border Using A and with RS facing, pick up and k 240 sts across top edge.

Row 1 (WS) P2, * k4, p4; rep from * to last 6 sts, k4, p2.

Row 2 K1, m1, k1, * p4, k4; rep from * to last 6 sts, p4, k1, m1, k1.

Cont in est rib pat, and inc 1 st at each end of needle every other row twice more—246 sts. Work 1 more WS row.

Change to B.

Row 1 (RS) K1, m1, k to last st, m1, k1—248 sts.

Row 2 P2, * k4, p4; rep from * to last 6 sts, k4, p2.

Bind off in rib pat.

Work bottom edge the same.

Using A and with RS facing, pick up and k 320 sts along one side edge, and work same as top border—328 sts.

Work other edge the same.

Sew corners together. Weave in all loose ends.

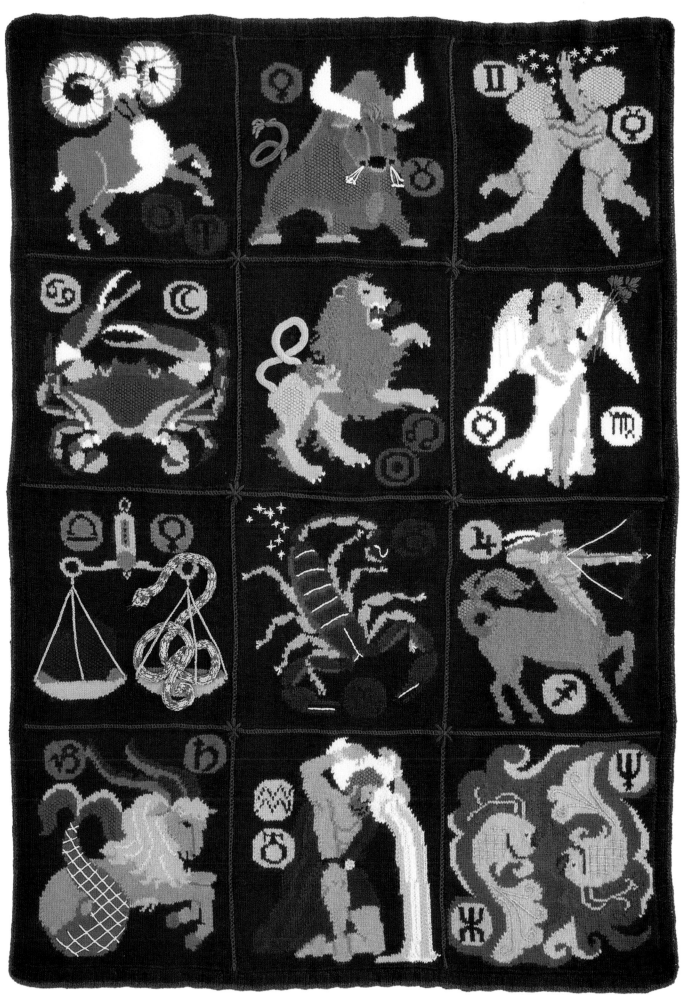

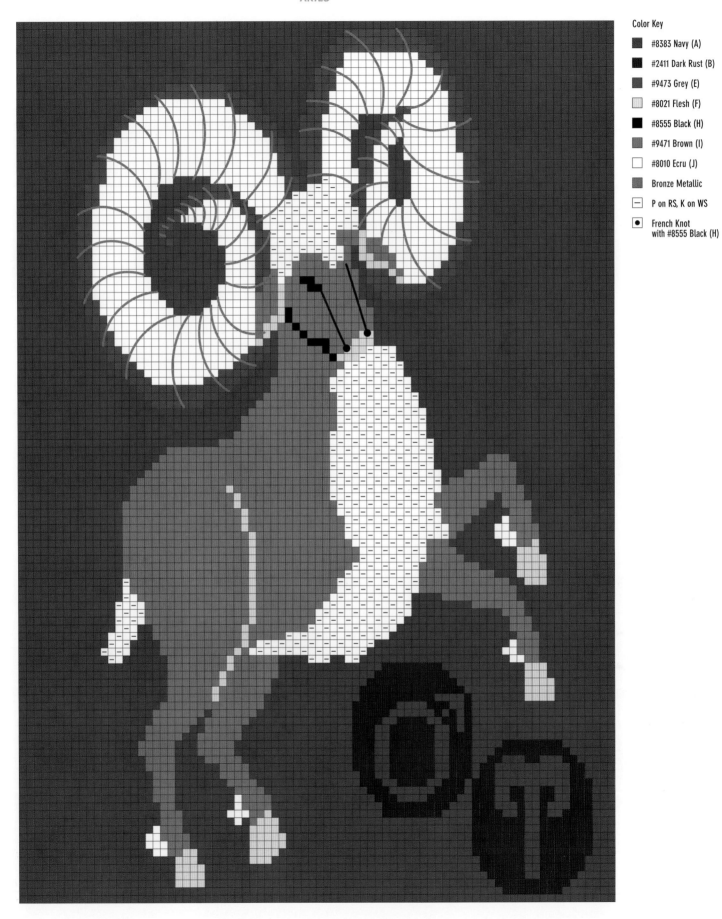

Color Key

- ■ #8383 Navy (A)
- ■ #2411 Dark Rust (B)
- ■ #9473 Grey (E)
- ▨ #8021 Flesh (F)
- ■ #8555 Black (H)
- ■ #9471 Brown (I)
- □ #8010 Ecru (J)
- ■ Bronze Metallic
- — P on RS, K on WS
- ● French Knot
  with #8555 Black (H)

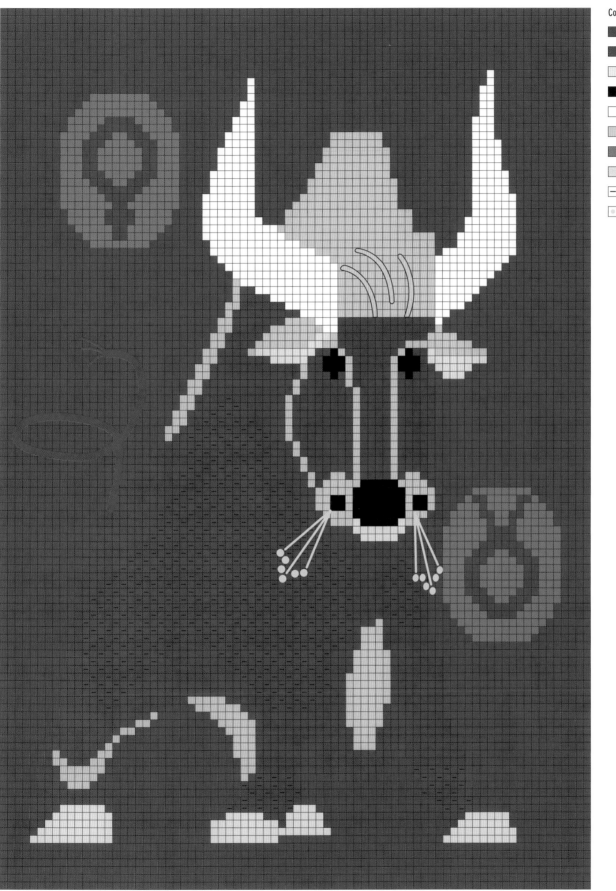

Color Key

■ #8383 Navy (A)

■ #9473 Grey (E)

☐ #8021 Flesh (F)

■ #8555 Black (H)

☐ #8010 Ecru (J) with White Metallic

▦ #7821 Taupe (K)

■ #9427 Teal (L)

☐ White Metallic

— P on RS, K on WS

⊙ French Knot
with White Metallic

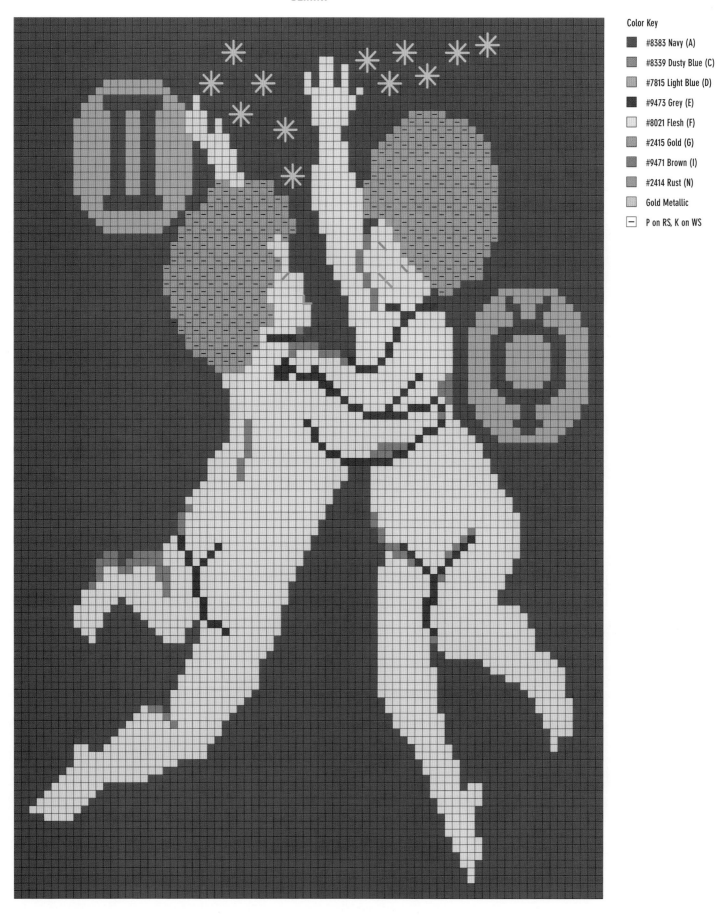

Color Key

- #8383 Navy (A)
- #8339 Dusty Blue (C)
- #7815 Light Blue (D)
- #9473 Grey (E)
- #8021 Flesh (F)
- #2415 Gold (G)
- #9471 Brown (I)
- #2414 Rust (N)
- Gold Metallic
- ⊟ P on RS, K on WS

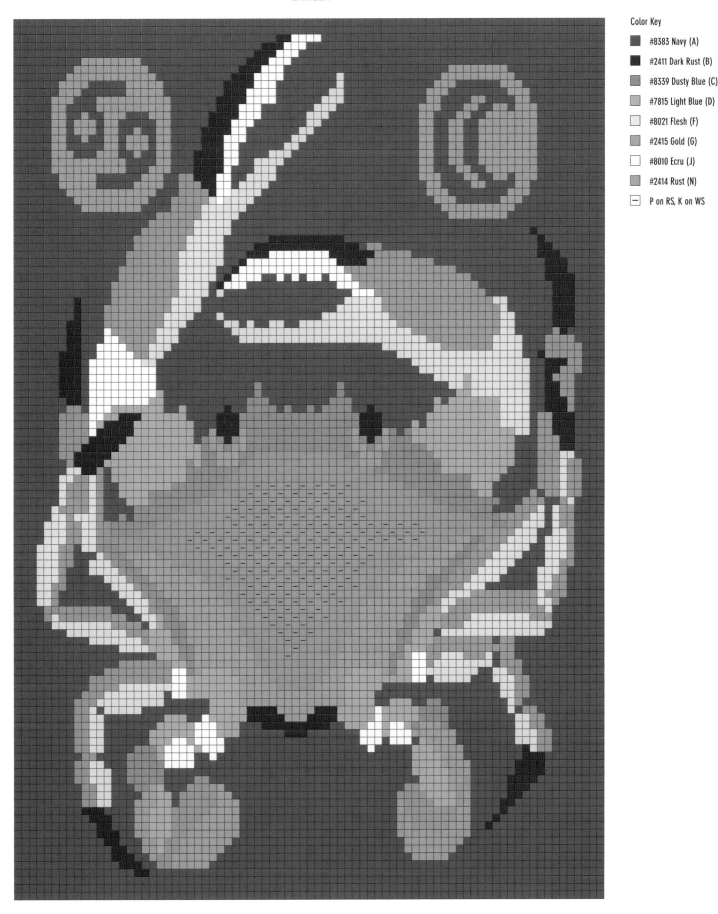

Color Key

■ #8383 Navy (A)

■ #2411 Dark Rust (B)

■ #8339 Dusty Blue (C)

■ #7815 Light Blue (D)

□ #8021 Flesh (F)

■ #2415 Gold (G)

□ #8010 Ecru (J)

■ #2414 Rust (N)

⊟ P on RS, K on WS

Color Key

■ #8383 Navy (A)

■ #9473 Grey (E)

▨ #2415 Gold (G)

■ Bark (H)

□ #8555 Black (H)

▨ #7821 Taupe (K)

▨ #2414 Rust (N)

✳ Bronze Metallic

— P on RS, K on WS

◘ Duplicate st in H

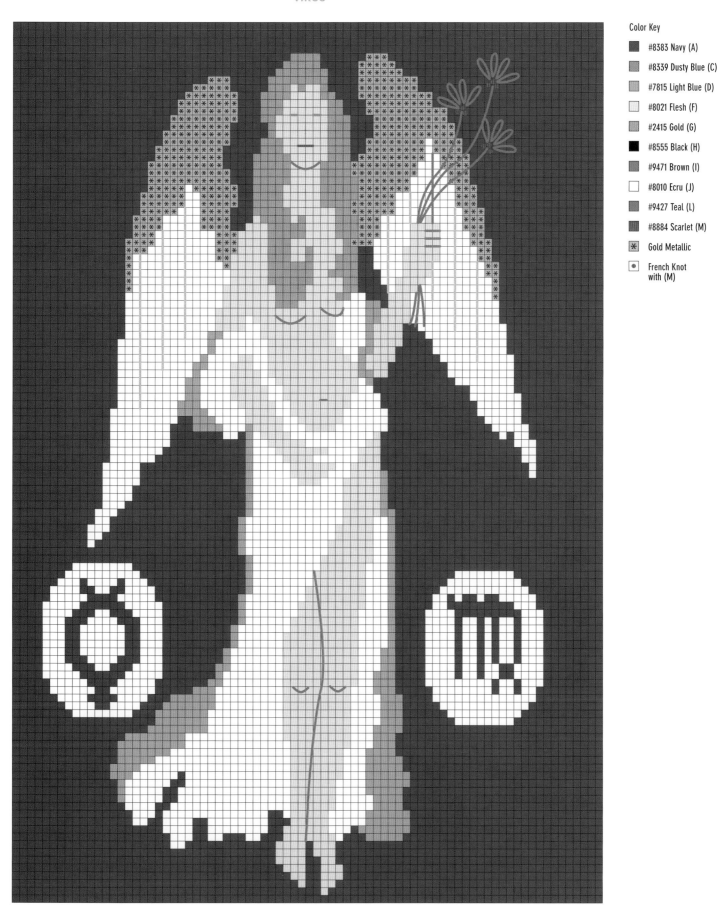

Color Key

- ■ #8383 Navy (A)
- ■ #8339 Dusty Blue (C)
- ■ #7815 Light Blue (D)
- □ #8021 Flesh (F)
- ■ #2415 Gold (G)
- ■ #8555 Black (H)
- ■ #9471 Brown (I)
- □ #8010 Ecru (J)
- ■ #9427 Teal (L)
- ▦ #8884 Scarlet (M)
- ✳ Gold Metallic
- ⊙ French Knot with (M)

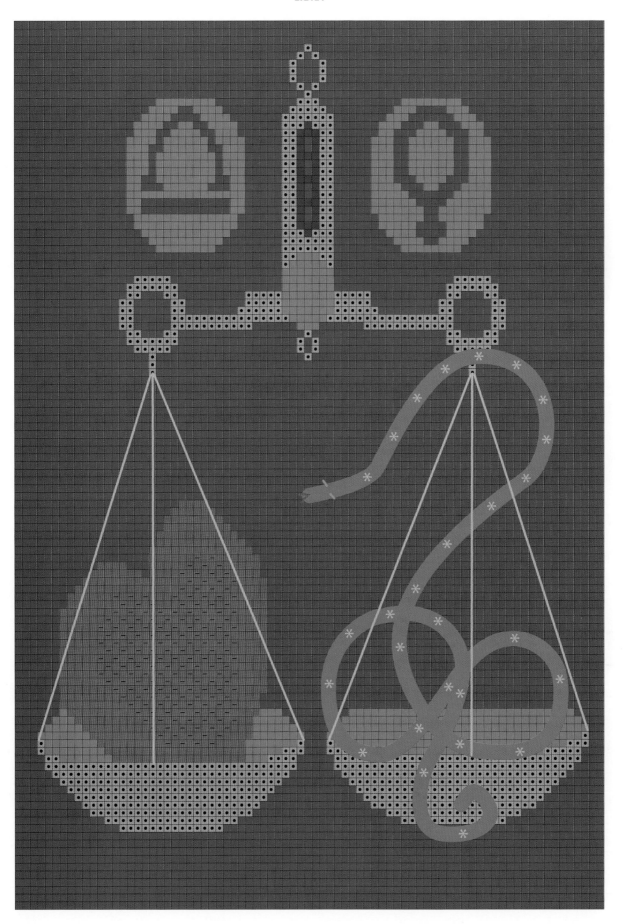

Color Key

■ #8383 Navy (A)

■ #9473 Grey (E)

▣ #2415 Gold (G)

▦ #9471 Brown (I)

■ #9427 Teal (L)

▥ #8884 Scarlet (M)

▦ #2414 Rust (N)

▦ Gold Metallic

⊟ P on RS, K on WS

✳ L and Gold Metallic
held tog (I-cord)

Color Key

■ #8383 Navy (A)
■ #2411 Dark Rust (B)
■ #8339 Dusty Blue (C)
□ #8021 Flesh (F)
■ #8884 Scarlet (M)
■ Silver Metallic

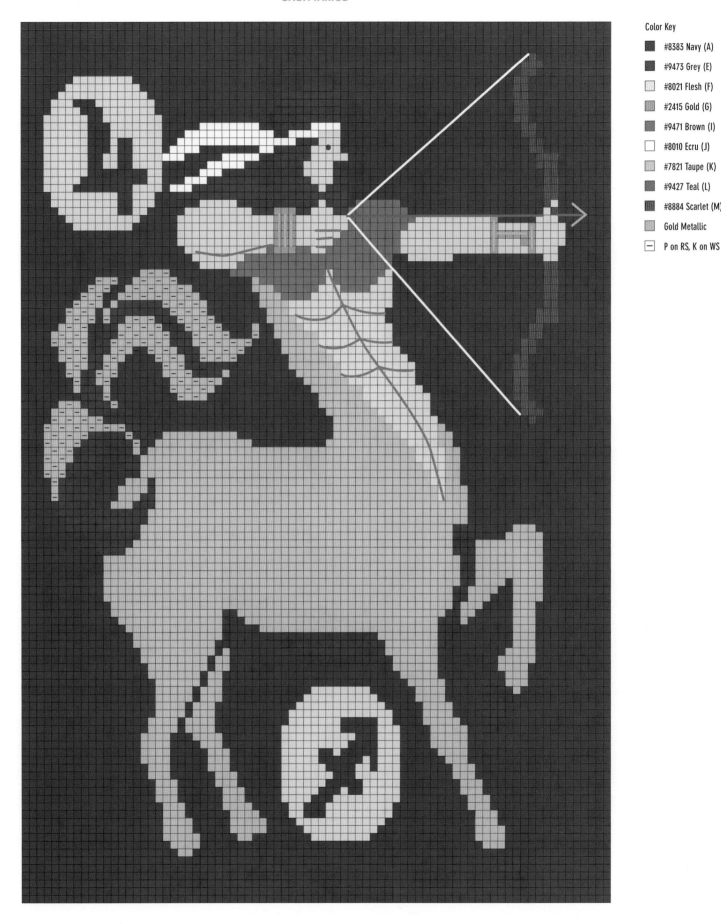

Color Key

- #8383 Navy (A)
- #9473 Grey (E)
- #8021 Flesh (F)
- #2415 Gold (G)
- #9471 Brown (I)
- #8010 Ecru (J)
- #7821 Taupe (K)
- #9427 Teal (L)
- #8884 Scarlet (M)
- Gold Metallic
- — P on RS, K on WS

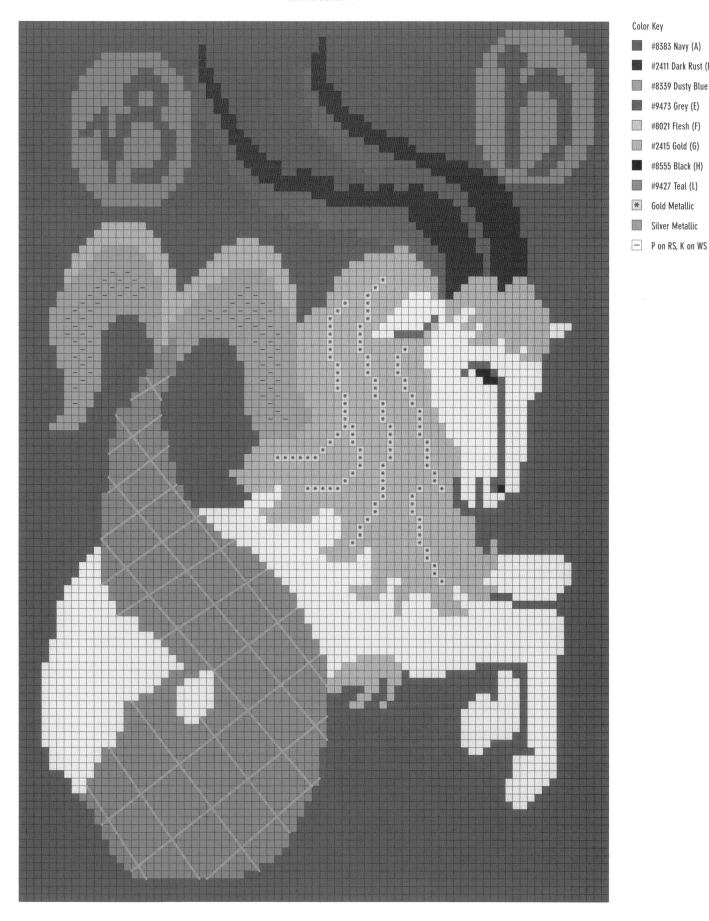

Color Key

- #8383 Navy (A)
- #2411 Dark Rust (B)
- #8339 Dusty Blue (C)
- #9473 Grey (E)
- #8021 Flesh (F)
- #2415 Gold (G)
- #8555 Black (H)
- #9427 Teal (L)
- ✳ Gold Metallic
- Silver Metallic
- — P on RS, K on WS

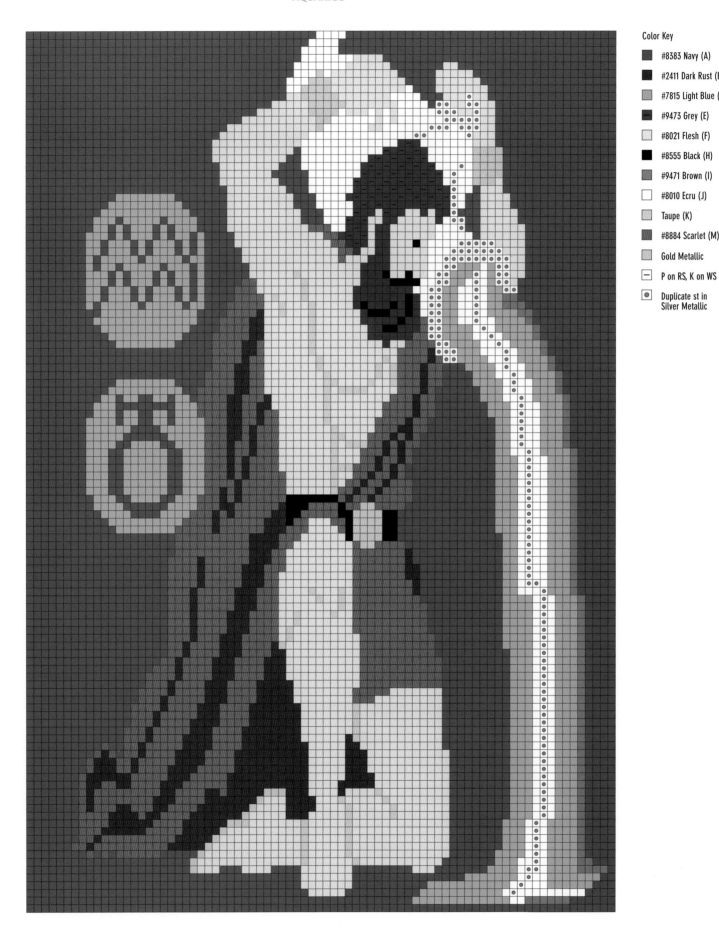

Color Key

- #8383 Navy (A)
- #2411 Dark Rust (B)
- #7815 Light Blue (D)
- #9473 Grey (E)
- #8021 Flesh (F)
- #8555 Black (H)
- #9471 Brown (I)
- #8010 Ecru (J)
- Taupe (K)
- #8884 Scarlet (M)
- Gold Metallic
- P on RS, K on WS
- Duplicate st in Silver Metallic

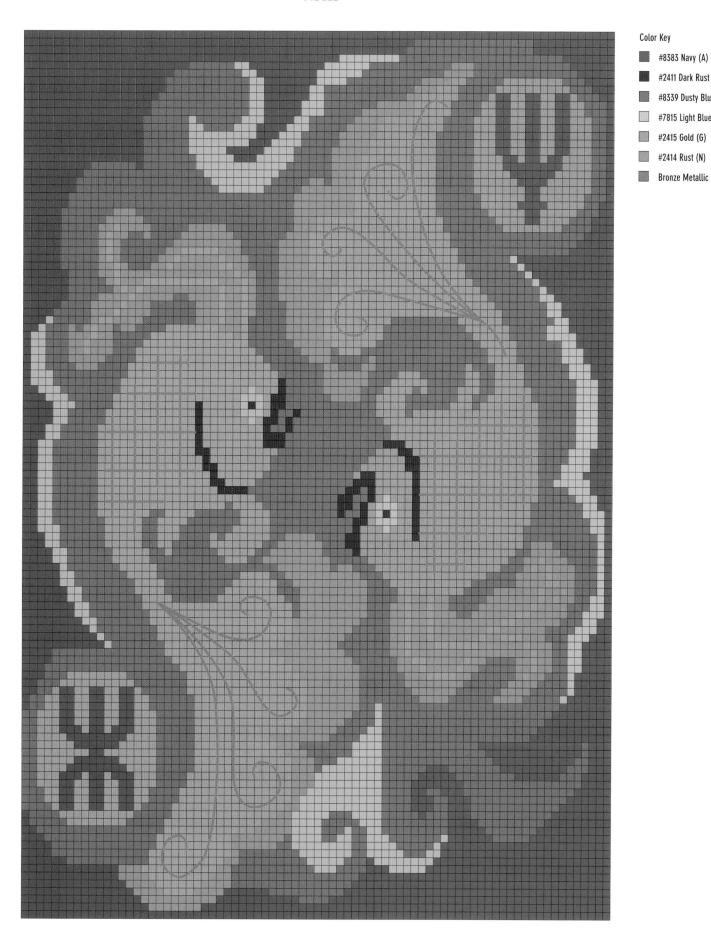

Color Key

■ #8383 Navy (A)

■ #2411 Dark Rust (B)

■ #8339 Dusty Blue (C)

□ #7815 Light Blue (D)

▨ #2415 Gold (G)

■ #2414 Rust (N)

■ Bronze Metallic

Trees Breeze

The design for this pattern has, over the years, become one of my most enduring showpieces; many fine knitters have made it, and I'm happy to include it in this collection. It is worked in one piece, and the tree and flower patterns repeat horizontally, starting and ending with the trees. It is bordered by a leaf stitch edging, knit and sewn around the afghan.

48" x 58"/122cm x 147cm

• 10 3oz/85g skeins (each approx 197yd/180m) of Lion Brand Yarn *Wool-Ease* (80% acrylic, 20% wool) in #99 fisherman
• Size U.S. 8 (5mm) circular needle (used as a straight needle), at least 36"/91.5cm length OR SIZE TO OBTAIN GAUGE
• Cable needle

18 sts and 26 rows = 4"/10cm over stockinette st.
TAKE TIME TO CHECK GAUGE.

SPECIAL STITCHES

4-st LC Sl 2 sts to cn and hold to front, k2, k2 from cn.

4-st RC Sl 2 sts to cn and hold to back, k2, k2 from cn.

2-st PLC Sl 1 st to cn and hold to front, p1, k1 from cn.

2-st PRC Sl 1 st to cn and hold to back, k1, p1 from cn.

3-st PLC Sl 2 sts to cn and hold to front, p1, k2 from cn.

3-st PRC Sl 1 st to cn and hold to back, k2, p1 from cn.

4-st PLC Sl 2 sts to cn and hold to front, p2, k2 from cn.

4-st PRC Sl 2 st to cn and hold to back, k2, p2 from cn.

TWIN TREES PATTERN

(multiple of 44 sts plus 4)

Rows 1, 3, 5, 7, 9, 11, 13, and 15 (WS) K4, * k12, p4, k8, p4, k16; rep from * to end.

Rows 2, 4, 6, 8, 10, 12 and 14 (RS) K the k sts, p the p sts.

Row 16 P4, * p12, m1, k4, p8, k4, m1, p16; rep from * to end—46 sts in each rep.

Row 17 and all rem odd rows K the k sts, p the p sts.

Row 18 P4, * p12, k1, m1, k4, p8, k4, m1, k1, p16; rep from * to end—48 sts in each rep.

Row 20 P4, * p10, 4-st PRC, k4, m1, p8, m1, k4, 4-st PLC, p14; rep from * to end—50 sts in each rep.

Row 22 P4, * p8, 4-st PRC, p2, k4, m1, k1, p8, k1, m1, k4, p2, 4-st PLC, p12; rep from * to end—52 sts in each rep.

Row 24 P4, * p6, 4-st PRC, p4, k4, 4-st PLC, p4, 4-st PRC, k4, p4, 4-st PLC, p10, rep from * to end.

Row 26 P4, * p5, 3-st PRC, p5, 3-st PRC, k2, p2, 4-st PLC, 4-st PRC, p2, k2, 3-st PLC, p5, 3-st PLC, p9; rep from * to end.

Row 28 P4, * p5, k2, p5, 3-st PRC, p1, 3-st PLC, p3, 4-st RC, p3, 3-st PRC, p1, 3-st PLC, p5, k2, p9; rep from * to end.

Row 30 P4, * p4, 2-st PRC, 2-st PLC, p3, 3-st PRC, p3, 3-st PLC, 4-st PRC, 4-st PLC, 3-st PRC, p3, 3-st PLC, p3, 2-st PRC, 2-st PLC, p8; rep from * to end.

Row 32 P4, * p3, 2-st PRC, p2, k1 tbl, p3, k2, p5, 4-st LC, p4, 4-st LC, p5, k2, p3, k1 tbl, p2, 2-st PLC, p7; rep from * to end.

Row 34 P4, * (p2, 2-st PRC) 3 times, 2-st PLC, p3, 3-st PRC, 3-st PLC, p2, 3-st PRC, 3-st PLC, p3, 2-st PRC, (2-st PLC, p2) 3 times, p4; rep from * to end.

Row 36 P4, * p5, (2-st PRC, p2) twice, k1 tbl, p3, k2, p2, 3-st PLC, 3-st PRC, p2, k2, p3, k1 tbl, (p2, 2-st PLC) twice, p9; rep from * to end.

Row 38 P4, * p4, (2-st PRC, p2) 3 times, 2-st PRC, 2-st PLC, p2, 4-st RC, p2, 2-st PRC, (2-st PLC, p2) 3 times, 2-st PLC, p8; rep from * to end.

Row 40 P4, * p3, 2-st PRC, p6, (2-st PRC, p2) twice, k1 tbl, p2, k4, p2, k1 tbl, (p2, 2-st PLC) twice, p6, 2-st PLC, p7; rep from * to end.

Row 42 P4, * p2, p2tog, p6, (2-st PRC, p2) 3 times, 4-st RC, (p2, 2-st PLC) 3 times, p6, p2tog tbl, p6; rep from * to end—50 sts in each rep.

Row 44 P4, * P8, 2-st PRC, p6, 2-st PRC, p1, 4-st

PRC, 4-st PLC, p1, 2-st PLC, p6, 2-st PLC, p12; rep from * to end.

Row 46 P4, * p7, p2tog, p6, 2-st PRC, p1, 2-st PRC, 2-st PLC, p2, 2-st PRC, 2-st PLC, p1, 2-st PLC, p6, p2tog tbl, p11; rep from * to end—48 sts in each rep.

Row 48 P4, * p13, 2-st PRC, p1, 2-st PRC, (p2, k1 tbl) twice, p2, 2-st PLC, p1, 2-st PLC, p17; rep from * to end.

Row 50 P4, * p12, p2tog, p1, (2-st PRC, p2) twice, 2-st PLC, p2, 2-st PLC, p1, p2tog tbl, p16; rep from * to end—46 sts in each rep.

Row 52 P4, * p17, 2-st PRC, p4, 2-st PLC, p21; rep from * to end.

Row 54 P4, * p17, k1 tbl, p6, k1 tbl, k21; rep from * to end.

Row 56 P4, * p16, p2tog, p6, p2tog tbl, p20; rep from * to end—44 sts in each rep.

Row 58 Purl.

DIVIDING PATTERN

(any number of sts)

Row 1 (RS) Knit.

Row 2 Purl.

Row 3 Knit.

Row 4–10 Purl.

Rows 11 and 13 Knit.

Rows 12 and 14 Purl.

FLOWER GARDEN PATTERN

(multiple of 12 sts plus 1)

Note: Always cast on 1 extra st before beginning this pattern, and k2tog on the last 2 sts of the final row.

Rows 1, 3, and 5 (RS) P12, * k1 tbl, p11; rep from * to last st, p1.

Rows 2, 4, 6, and 8 K12, * p1 tbl, k11; rep from * to last st, k1.

Row 7 P8, * insert tip of right needle front to back into the fabric at right of twisted st of row 1, pull up a long, loose loop, k1, pass loop over k st, p3,

k1 tbl, p3, pull up another loop at left of same st of row 1, k1, pass loop over k st, p3; rep from * to last 5 sts, p5.

Row 9 P12, * (k1, yo) 3 times and k1 all in next st, p11; rep from * to last st, p1—18 sts in each rep.

Row 10 K12, * p7, k11; rep from * to last st, k1.

Row 11 P12, * k2tog tbl, k3tog tbl, k2tog tbl, p11; rep from * to last st, p1—14 sts in each rep.

Row 12 K12, * p3tog, k11; rep from * to last st, k1—12 sts in each rep.

Rows 13, 15, and 17 P6, * k1 tbl, p11; rep from * to last 7 sts, k1 tbl, p6.

Rows 14, 16, and 18 K6, * p1 tbl, k11; rep from * to last 7 sts, p1 tbl, k6.

Row 19 P2, * pull up a loop as before at right of twisted st of row 13, k1, pass loop over k st, p3, k1 tbl, p3, pull up another loop at left of same st of row 13, k1, pass loop over k st, p3; rep from * to end, eliminating last p.

Row 20 K6, * p1 tbl, k11; rep from * to last 7 sts, p1 tbl, k6.

Row 21 P6, * (k1, yo) 3 times and k1 all in next st, p11; rep from * to last 7 sts, (k1, yo) 3 times and k1 all in next st, p6—18 sts in each rep.

Row 22 K6, * p7, k11; rep from * to last 13 sts, p7, k6.

Row 23 P6, * k2tog tbl, k3tog tbl, k2tog tbl, p11; rep from * to last 13 sts, k2tog tbl, k3tog tbl, k2tog tbl, p6—14 sts in each rep.

Row 24 K6, * p3tog, k11; rep from * to last 9 sts, p3tog, k6—12 sts in each rep.

Rep rows 1–24 once more.

AFGHAN

Cast on 180 sts, and work 2 rows in stockinette st.

Work next 58 rows in twin trees pat.

Work next 14 rows in dividing pat.

Work next 48 rows in flower garden pat.

Work next 14 rows in dividing pat.

Work next 58 rows in twin trees pat.

Work next 14 rows in dividing pat.

Work next 48 rows in flower garden pat.

Work next 14 rows in dividing pat.

Work next 58 rows in twin trees pat.

Bind off.

FINISHING

Tulip-bud border Cast on 8 sts.

Row 1 (RS) K5, yo, k1, yo, k2—10 sts.

Row 2 P6, kfb, k3—11 sts.

Row 3 K4, p1, k2, yo, k1, yo, k3—13 sts.

Row 4 P8, kfb, k4—14 sts.

Row 5 K4, p2, k3, yo, k1, yo, k4—16 sts.

Row 6 P10, kfb, k5—17 sts.

Row 7 K4, p3, k4, yo, k1, yo, k5—19 sts.

Row 8 P12, kfb, k6—20 sts.

Row 9 K4, p4, ssk, k7, k2tog, k1—18 sts.

Row 10 P10, kfb, k7—19 sts.

Row 11 K4, p5, ssk, k5, k2tog, k1—17 sts.

Row 12 P8, kfb, k2, p1, k5—18 sts.

Row 13 K4, p1, k1, p4, ssk, k3, k2tog, k1—16 sts.

Row 14 P6, kfb, k3, p1, k5—17 sts.

Row 15 K4, p1, k1, p5, ssk, k1, k2tog, k1—15 sts.

Row 16 P4, kfb, k4, p1, k5—16 sts.

Row 17 K4, p1, k1, p6, sk2p, k1—14 sts.

Row 18 P2tog, bind off 5 sts, p3, k4—8 sts.

Rep rows 1–18 until border fits around afghan (approx 212"/538cm). Bind off.

Sew border around afghan.

Weave in all loose ends.

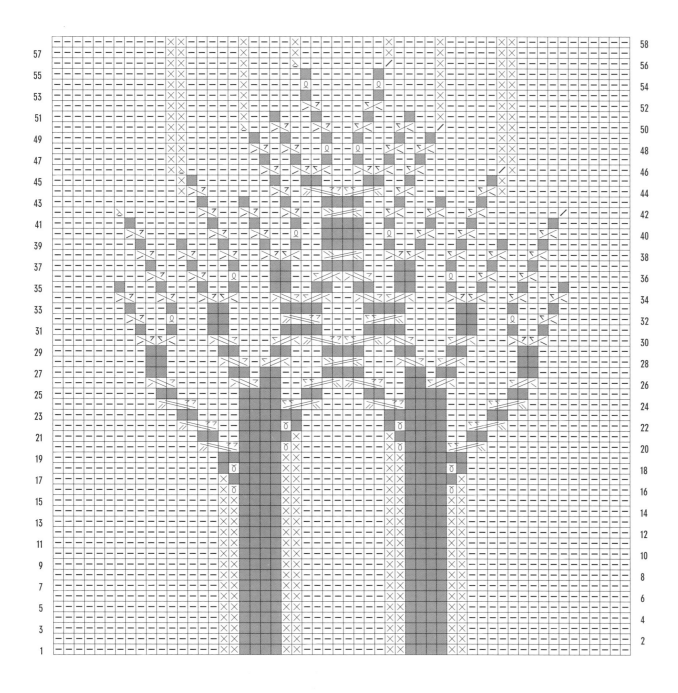

Stitch Key

⊠	No st			4-st LC
—	P1 on RS rows, k1 on WS rows			4-st RC
▨	K 1 on RS rows, p1 on WS rows			2-st PLC
ʊ	M1			2-st PRC
╱	P2 tog			3-st PLC
⊠	P2tog tbl			3-st PRC
Ω	K1 tbl			4-st PLC
				4-st PRC

Proposal Sampler

This truly is a gift from the heart. The entire afghan is worked in intarsia from multiple charts (this definitely is not a first-time colorwork project). When it was first published, I classified this on my knitting difficulty scale as "suicidal." But go ahead and take it on—it makes a wonderful heirloom for a loved one, especially for a family member's wedding. An alphabet is included in duplicate stitch to personalize with a name.

45" x 57"/114cm x 144.5cm

• 4 (1¾oz/50 g) skeins (each approx 191yd/175m) of Rowan/Westminster fibers, Inc., *Felted Tweed* (50% merino wool, 25% alpaca, 25% viscose), in #159 Carbon (A) and #147 Dragon (C)
• 3 skeins in #156 Wheat (B)
• 1 skein in #157 Camel (U)
• 1 (1¾oz/50g) skeins (each approx 137 yd/125m) RYC/Westminster Fibers, Inc., *Pure Wool* DK (100% superwash wool) in #013 Enamel (D), #004 Black (E), #014 Hay (F), #020 Parsley (G), #019 Avocado (H), #023 Shamrock (I), #017 Mocha (J), #016 Hessian (K), #015 Barley (L), #007 Cypress (M), #006 Pier (N), #008 Marine (O), #039 Lavender (P), #030 Damson (Q), #029 Pomgranate (R), #028 Raspberry (S) and #032 Gilt (T)
• Size U.S. 6 (4mm) circular needle (used as a straight needle), at least 36"/91.5cm length OR SIZE TO OBTAIN GAUGE
• Yarn bobbins
• Yarn needle
• Fabric for backing (optional)

22 sts and 30 rows = 4"/10cm over stockinette st.
TAKE TIME TO CHECK GAUGE.

Chart 1 Borders (pages 126-127)
Chart 2 Bottom panel (pages 128-131)
Chart 3 Center panel (pages 132-133)
Chart 4 Top panel (pages 134-135)
Chart 5 Top corners (pages 136-137)

Using A, cast on 230 sts.
Row 1 (RS) K1, m1, k to last 2 sts, m1, k1.
Row 2 Purl.
Rep rows 1 and 2 twice more—236 sts.
Knit 2 rows for turning ridge. Cont in stockinette st, working charts as follows:
Next row (RS) Work 38 sts of chart 1 (bottom) in reverse, then 160 sts of chart 2, then 38 sts of chart 1.
Cont as est until chart 1 is complete, working chart 3 for middle and chart 4 for top after chart 2 (bottom) is finished.
Next row (RS) Work 38 sts cont chart 1 in reverse, then 160 sts of chart 3, then 38 sts cont chart 1.
Cont as est until chart 1 (top) is complete and ending 26 rows from top of chart 4.
Next row (RS) Work 38 sts of chart 5, then 160 sts cont chart 4, then 38 sts of chart 5 in reverse.
Cont as est until chart 4 is complete.
Next row (RS) Work 118 sts cont chart 5, then 118 sts cont chart 5 in reverse.
Cont as est until chart 5 is complete.
Knit 2 rows for turning ridge.
Next 2 rows:
Row 1 (RS) K1, ssk, k to last 3 sts, k2tog, k1.
Row 2 Purl.
Rep rows 1 and 2 twice more—230 sts.
Bind off.

Name and date Using E, work in duplicate st.
Flower centers Using L, S or G as indicated, work straight st.
Skirt (chart 2) Using M, work stem st.
Skirt (chart 4) Using Q and R, work Jacobean couching.
Sun rays Using T, work straight st.
Bouquet (chart 2) Using H, work straight st for stems. Using D, work French knots for flowers.
Bouquet (chart 4) Using G, work straight st for stems. Using Q, work French knots for flowers.
Facial features Using K and S, work short straight sts.
Harp strings & arrow Using J or L as indicated, work in stem st.
Birds' and ducks' eyes using K or L as indicated, work French knots.

Side hems Using A and with RS facing, pick up and k 285 sts along one side edge.
Knit 1 row for turning ridge.
Next 2 rows:
Row 1 (RS) K1, ssk, k to last 3 sts, k2tog, k1.
Row 2 Purl.
Rep rows 1 and 2 twice more—279 sts. Bind off.
Work other edge the same.
Assembly Fold hems to WS and sew down.
Weave in all loose ends.
Sew backing fabric if desired.

ABCDEFGHIJKLMN
OPQRSTUVWXYZ
1234567890

MARY AND JOHN SMITH
AUGUST 3 1999

CHART 1 (SIDE PANELS)

TOP

MIDDLE

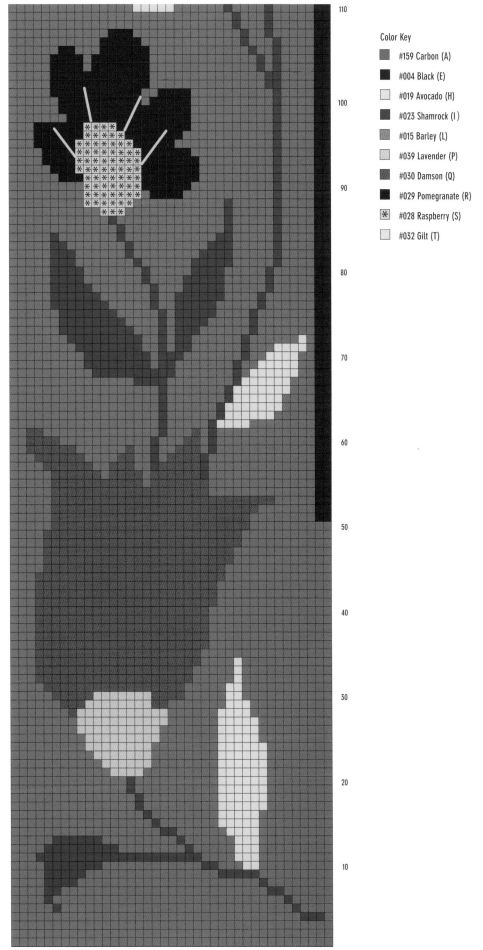

Color Key

■ #159 Carbon (A)
■ #004 Black (E)
□ #019 Avocado (H)
■ #023 Shamrock (I)
■ #015 Barley (L)
□ #039 Lavender (P)
■ #030 Damson (Q)
■ #029 Pomegranate (R)
⊛ #028 Raspberry (S)
□ #032 Gilt (T)

110

100

90

80

70

60

50

40

30

20

10

BOTTOM

CHART 2 (BOTTOM PANEL)

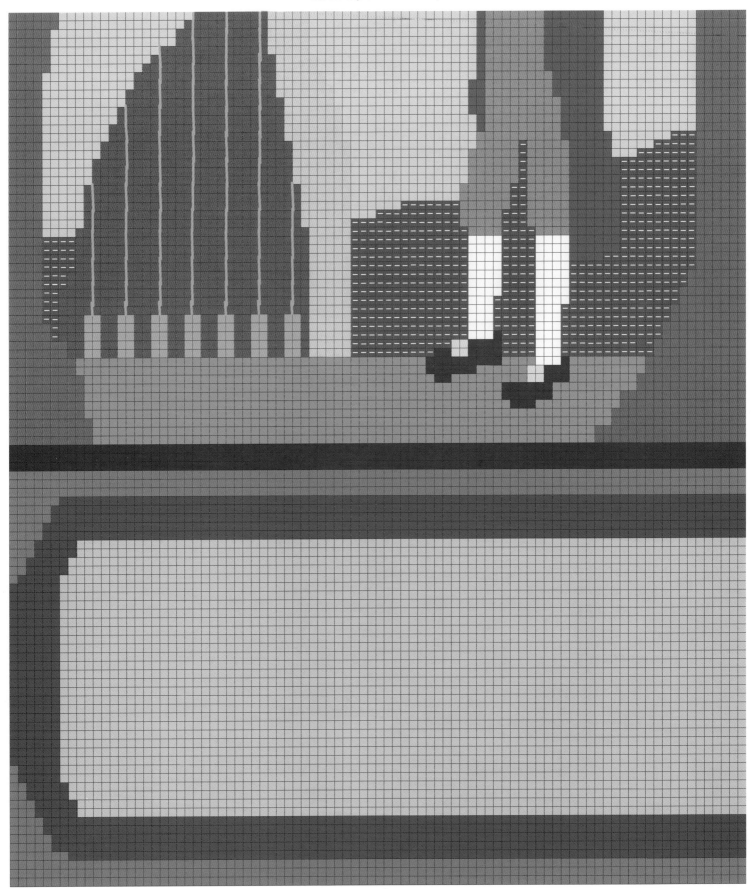

160 sts

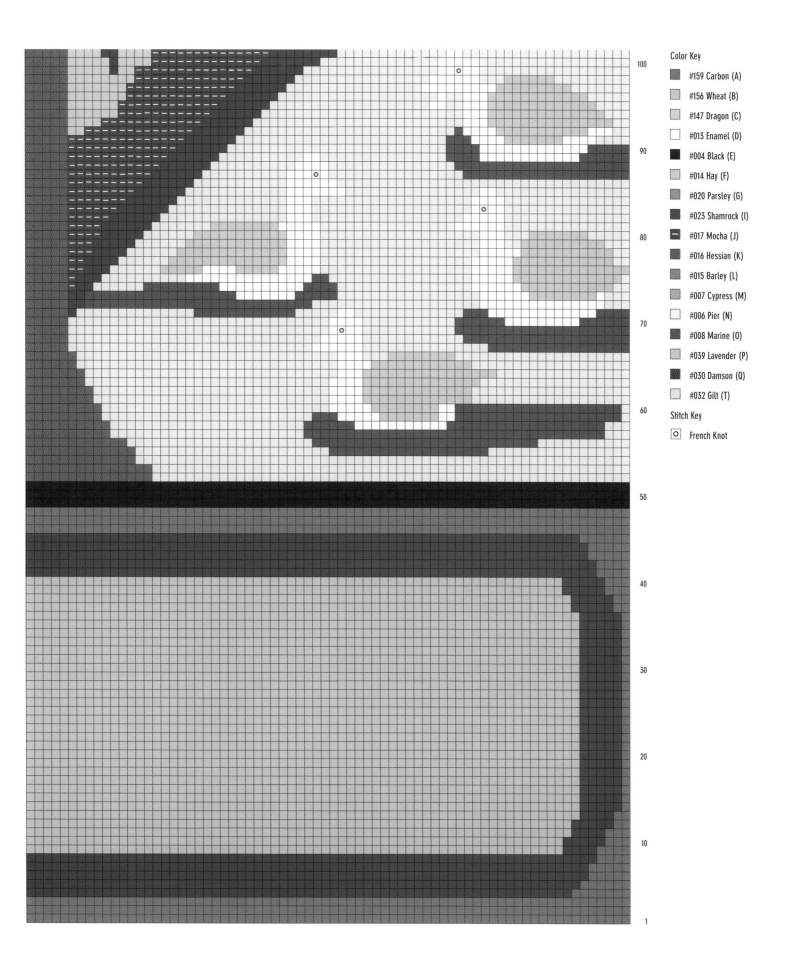

Color Key

- ■ #159 Carbon (A)
- ■ #156 Wheat (B)
- ■ #147 Dragon (C)
- □ #013 Enamel (D)
- ■ #004 Black (E)
- ■ #014 Hay (F)
- ■ #020 Parsley (G)
- ■ #023 Shamrock (I)
- ▬ #017 Mocha (J)
- ▨ #016 Hessian (K)
- ■ #015 Barley (L)
- ■ #007 Cypress (M)
- □ #006 Pier (N)
- ■ #008 Marine (O)
- ■ #039 Lavender (P)
- ■ #030 Damson (Q)
- ▨ #032 Gilt (T)

Stitch Key

- ⊙ French Knot

CHART 2 (BOTTOM PANEL)

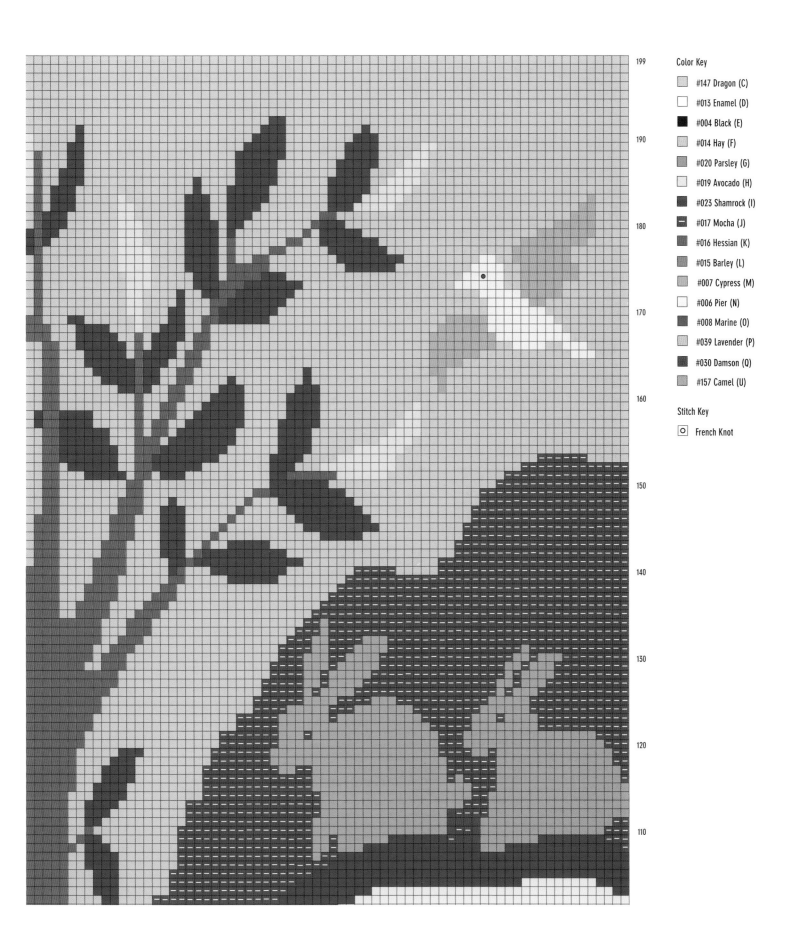

Color Key

☐ #147 Dragon (C)

☐ #013 Enamel (D)

■ #004 Black (E)

☐ #014 Hay (F)

☐ #020 Parsley (G)

☐ #019 Avocado (H)

■ #023 Shamrock (I)

▦ #017 Mocha (J)

☐ #016 Hessian (K)

☐ #015 Barley (L)

☐ #007 Cypress (M)

☐ #006 Pier (N)

■ #008 Marine (O)

☐ #039 Lavender (P)

■ #030 Damson (Q)

☐ #157 Camel (U)

Stitch Key

⊙ French Knot

199
190
180
170
160
150
140
130
120
110

CHART 3 (CENTER PANEL)

160 sts

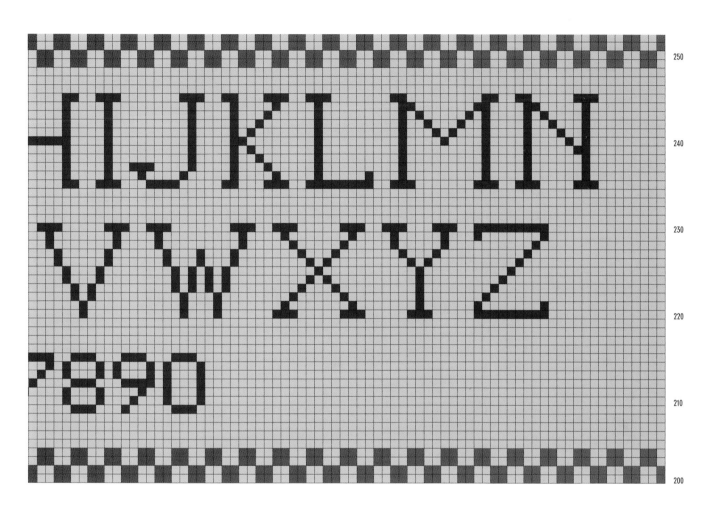

250

240

230

220

210

200

Color Key

#156 Wheat (B)

#004 Black (E)

#016 Hessian (K)

CHART 4 (TOP PANEL)

Color Key

#156 Wheat (B)	#004 Black (E)	#019 Avocado (H)	#016 Hessian (K)	#006 Pier (N)
#147 Dragon (C)	#014 Hay (F)	#023 Shamrock (I)	#015 Barley (L)	#008 Marine (O)
#013 Enamel (D)	#020 Parsley (G)	#017 Mocha (J)	#007 Cypress (M)	#039 Lavender (P)

351
350

340

330

320

310

300

290

280

270

260

Stitch Key

■ #030 Damson (Q)   ▫ #032 Gilt (T)   ⊠ Jacobean Couching

■ #029 Pomegranate (R)   ■ #157 Camel (U)   ⊙ French Knot

✳ #028 Raspberry (S)

CHART 5 TOP CORNERS

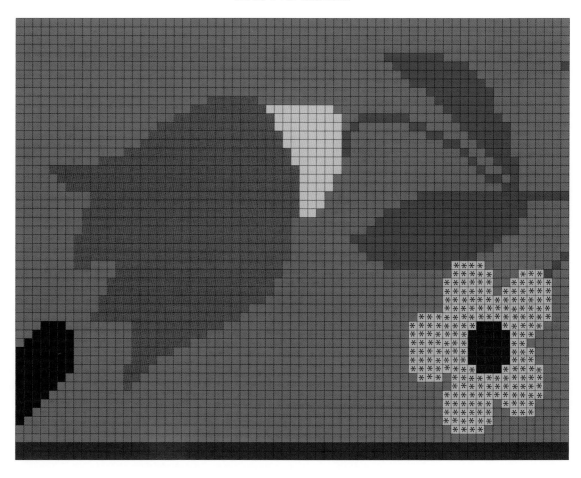

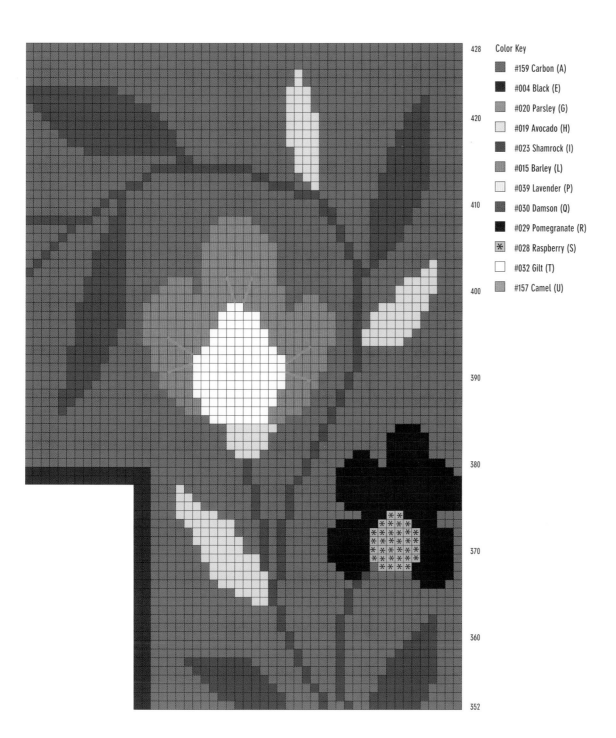

428

420

410

400

390

380

370

360

352

Color Key

#159 Carbon (A)

#004 Black (E)

#020 Parsley (G)

#019 Avocado (H)

#023 Shamrock (I)

#015 Barley (L)

#039 Lavender (P)

#030 Damson (Q)

#029 Pomegranate (R)

#028 Raspberry (S)

#032 Gilt (T)

#157 Camel (U)

White Sampler

This white-on-white afghan is composed of nine blocks, each worked in different

pattern stitches. A variety of appliqué stitches, fringes and embroidery is sewn onto

each block for overall interest and depth. I've always enjoyed working with white-

on-white appliqués for a multidimensional look.

KNITTED MEASUREMENTS

45" x 59"/114cm x 150cm

MATERIALS

- 19 3oz/85g skeins (each approx 197yd/180m) of Lion Brand Yarn *Wool-Ease* (80% acrylic, 20% wool) in #99 fisherman
- Size U.S. 8 (5mm) circular needle (used as a straight needle), at least 36"/91.5cm length OR SIZE TO OBTAIN GAUGE
- Set of double pointed needles in same size (for I-cords and tubes)
- Size F/5 (3.75mm) crochet hook
- Cable needle (cn)
- Yarn needle

GAUGE

18 sts and 28 rows = 4"/10cm over stockinette st.
TAKE TIME TO CHECK GAUGE.

SPECIAL STITCHES

RT Knit 2nd st on needle without dropping off, then knit 1st st, then drop off both.

LT Knit 2nd st on needle tbl without dropping off, then knit 1st st, then drop off both.

T2 Wyib, insert right needle purlwise into 1st st, knit 2nd st, then knit 1st st tbl.

4-st RC Sl 2 sts to cn and hold to back, k2, k2 from cn.

4-st LC Sl 2 sts to cn and hold to front, k2, k2 from cn.

Make bobble—Kfb twice and k1 all into next st—5 sts, turn and purl, turn and knit, turn and purl, turn and pass 2nd, 3rd, 4th, and 5th sts over 1st—1 st.

TUBE ST

(5 sts)
Row 1 K1 (sl1, k1) twice.
Row 2 Sl1, (p1, sl1) twice.
Rep rows 1 and 2 for tube st.

SEED ST

(odd number of sts)
Every row K1, * p1, k1; rep from * to end.

REVERSE STOCKINETTE ST

(any number of sts)
Row 1 (RS) Purl.
Row 2 Knit.
Rep rows 1 and 2 for reverse stockinette st.

K5, P5 RIB PATTERN

(multiple of 10 sts)
Every row * K5, p5, rep from * to end.

SQUARE 1 (TOP LEFT)

Cast on 61 sts.
Rows 1–8 Work in stockinette st, beg on a RS row.
Rows 9 and 10 Knit.
Rep rows 1-10 until piece measures 14"/35.5cm.
Bind off.

Trees

(make 2)
Cast on 7 sts.
Rows 1, 3, and 5 K1, * p1, k1; rep from * to end.
Row 2 and 4 P1, * k1, p1; rep from * to end.
Row 6 K1, * p1, k1; rep from * to end, cast on 12 sts using the cable cast on—19 sts.
Row 7 Knit to end, cast on 12 sts using the cable cast on—31 sts.
Row 8 Purl.
Row 9 K13, ssk, yo, k1, yo, k2tog, k13.
Even rows 10–24 Purl.
Row 11 K1, ssk, k10, ssk, yo, k1, yo, k2tog, k10, k2tog, k1—29 sts.
Row 13 K1, ssk, k9, ssk, yo, k1, yo, k2tog, k9, k2tog, k1—27 sts.
Row 15 K1, ssk, k8, ssk, yo, k1, yo, k2tog, k8, k2tog, k1—25 sts.
Row 17 K1, ssk, k7, ssk, yo, k1, yo, k2tog, k7, k2tog, k1—23 sts.
Row 19 K1, ssk, k6, ssk, yo, k1, yo, k2tog, k6, k2tog, k1—21 sts.
Row 21 K1, ssk, k5, ssk, yo, k1, yo, k2tog, k5, k2tog, k1—19 sts.
Row 23 K1, ssk, k4, ssk, yo, k1, yo, k2tog, k4, k2tog, k1—17 sts.

Row 25 K1, ssk, k3, ssk, yo, k1, yo, k2tog, k3, k2tog, k1—15 sts.

Row 26 P to end, cast on 6 sts using the cable cast on—21 sts.

Row 27 K11, ssk, yo, k1 yo, k2tog, k5, cast on 6 sts using the cable cast on—27 sts.

Even rows 28-40 Purl.

Row 29-39 As rows 15-25.

Row 41 K1, ssk, k2, ssk, yo, k1, yo, k2tog, k2, k2tog, k1—13 sts.

Row 42 P to end, cast on 4 sts using the cable cast on—17 sts.

Row 43 K8, ssk, yo, k1, yo, k2tog, k4, cast on 4 sts using the cable cast on—21 sts.

Even rows 44–62 Purl.

Row 45-49 As rows 21-25.

Row 51 As row 41.

Row 53 K1, ssk, k1, ssk, yo, k1, yo, k2tog, k1, k2tog, k1—11 sts.

Row 55 K1, ssk twice, yo, k1, yo, k2tog, twice, k1—9 sts.

Row 57 K1, ssk, k3, k2tog, k1—7 sts.

Row 59 K1, ssk, k1, k2tog, k1—5 sts.

Row 61 Ssk, k1, k2tog—3 sts.

Row 63 Sk2p.

Fasten off.

Sew trees onto square as shown in photo.

SQUARE 2

Cast on 67 sts.

Row 1 (RS) K1 (selvage), * work 13 sts in seed st, work 13 sts in stockinette st; rep from * once more, work 13 sts in seed st, k1 (selvage).

Cont in est pats for 17 more rows.

Row 19 K1 (selvage), * work 13 sts in stockinette st, work 13 sts in seed st; rep from * once more, work 13 sts in stockinette st, k1 (selvage).

Cont in est pats for 17 more rows.

Rep rows 1–36 once more, then rows 1–18 once more. Bind off.

Attach 1¼"/3cm fringes around the borders of 2 seed st blocks.

SQUARE 3

Cast on 70 sts.

Rows 1, 3, and 5 (WS) K3, * p4, k2, p2, k2; rep from * to last 7 sts, p4, k3.

Row 2 P3, * 4-st LC, p2, T2, p2; rep from * to last 7 sts, 4-st LC, p3.

Rows 4 and 6 P3, * k4, p2 T2, p2; rep from * to last 7 sts, k4, p3.

Rep rows 1–6 until piece measures 14"/35.5cm, ending on a row 4.

Bind off.

SQUARE 4

Cast on 74 sts.

Row 1 (RS) K1, * LT, k4, RT; rep from * to last st, k1.

Row 2 and all even rows Purl.

Row 3 K2, * LT, k2, RT, k2; rep from * to end.

Row 5 K3, * LT, RT, k4; rep from * to last 7 sts, LT, RT, k3.

Row 7 K4, * RT, k6; rep from * to last 6 sts, RT, k4.

Row 9 K3, * RT, LT, k4; rep from * to last 7 sts, RT, LT, k3.

Row 11 K2, * RT, k2, LT, k2; rep from * to end.

Row 13 K1, * RT, k4, LT; rep from * to last st, k1.

Row 15 K8, * LT, k6; rep from * to last 2 sts, k2.

Row 16 As row 2.

Rep rows 1–16 until piece measures 14"/35.5cm ending on a row 8 or 16.

Bind off.

Heart

Cast on 3 sts. Using a separate ball of yarn, cast

on another 3 sts.

Work both sets simultaneously as follows:

Row 1 (RS) K1, m1, k1, m1, k1—5 sts in each set.

Row 2 and all even rows Purl.

Rows 3, 5, and 7 K1, m1, k to last st, m1, k1—11 sts in each set.

Row 9 K1, m1, k9, k2tog (joining the 2 sets), k9, m1, k1—23 sts.

Row 11 Knit.

Odd rows 13–31 K1, ssk, k to last 3 sts, k2tog, k1—21 sts.

Row 33 Sk2p.

Fasten off.

Ruffle

Cast on 72 sts.

Row 1 (WS) * K1, p1; rep from * to end.

Row 2 * K1, m1, p1; rep from * to end—108 sts.

Row 3 * K1, p2; rep from * to end.

Row 4 * K2, m1, p1; rep from * to end—144 sts.

Row 5 * K1, p3; rep from * to end.

Row 6 * K3, m1, p1; rep from * to end—180 sts.

Row 7 * K1, p4; rep from * to end.

Row 8 * K4, m1, p1; rep from * to end—216 sts.

Row 9 * K1, p5; rep from * to end.

Row 10 * K5, m1, p1; rep from * to end—252 sts.

Bind off.

Sew side edges of ruffle together, then sew cast on row to outer edge of heart.

Sew heart onto square as shown in photo.

SQUARE 5

Center panel

Cast on 24 sts, and work in stockinette st until piece measures 14"/35.5cm.

Bind off.

Side panels

(make 2)

Cast on 23 sts.

Row 1 and all odd rows (WS) K2, * p5, k2; rep from * to end.

Row 2 P2, * LT, k3, p2; rep from * to end.

Row 4 P2, * k1, LT, k2, p2; rep from * to end.

Row 6 P2, * k2, LT, k1, p2; rep from * to end.

Row 8 P2, * k3, LT, p2; rep from * to end.

Rep rows 1-8 until piece measures 14"/35.5cm.

Bind off.

Paisleys

(make 3)

Cast on 5 sts, and work in tube st until piece measures 9"/23cm.

Bind off.

Bobbles

(make 3)

Cast on 1 st, make bobble, then fasten off.

Coil paisley tubes and sew tubes and bobbles to center panel as shown in photo.

Work 12 French knots around each paisley.

Sew a side panel on either side of the center panel.

SQUARE 6

Cast on 62 sts, and work in reverse stockinette st until piece measures 14"/35.5cm.

Bind off.

Flower

Cast on 58 sts.

Row 1 (RS) K3, * yo, k2, ssk, k2tog, k2, yo, k1; rep from * to last st, k1.

Even rows 2–6 Purl.

Row 3 K2, * yo, k2, ssk, k2tog, k2, yo, k1; rep from * to last 2 sts, k2.

Row 5 As row 1.

Row 7 * K1, k3tog; rep from * to last 2 sts, k2—30 sts.

Row 8 * P1, p3tog; rep from * to last 2 sts, p2—

16 sts.

Cut yarn, and use a yarn needle to slide tail through rem sts. Pull tight.

Leaves

(make 3)

Cast on 5 sts.

Row 1 (RS) K2, yo, k1, yo, k2—7 sts.

Even rows 2-16 Purl.

Row 3 K3, yo, k1, yo, k3—9 sts.

Row 5 K4, yo, k1, yo, k4—11 sts.

Row 7 K5, yo, k1, yo, k5—13 sts.

Row 9 Ssk, k9, k2tog—11 sts.

Row 11 Ssk, k7, k2tog—9 sts.

Row 13 Ssk, k5, k2tog—7 sts.

Row 15 Ssk, k3, k2tog—5 sts.

Row 17 Ssk, k1, k2tog—3 sts.

Row 18 P3tog.

Fasten off.

Work in chain st across square, making 3 vertical lines and 3 horizontal lines, evenly spaced.

Sew flower and leaves onto square as shown in photo.

SQUARE 7

Cast on 62 sts.

Row 1 (RS) K1, * p12, k2tog, yo, k2; rep from * to last 13 sts, p12, k1.

Row 2 K1, * k12, p2tog, yo, p2; rep from * to last 13 sts, k13.

Rep rows 1 and 2 until piece measures 14"/35.5cm ending on a row 2.

Bind off.

Sunflower center

Cast on 125 sts.

Row 1 (WS) Purl.

Row 2 * K2, make bobble; rep from * to last 2 sts, k2.

Bind off.

Petals

(make 9)

Cast on 5 sts.

Row 1 (RS) K2, yo, k1, yo, k2—7 sts.

Even rows 2-20 Purl.

Row 3 K3, yo, k1, yo, k3—9 sts.

Row 5 K4, yo, k1, yo, k4—11 sts.

Row 7 K5, yo, k1, yo, k5—13 sts.

Row 9 K6, yo, k1, yo, k6—15 sts.

Row 11 Ssk, k11, k2tog—13 sts.

Row 13 Ssk, k9, k2tog—11 sts.

Row 15 Ssk, k7, k2tog—9 sts.

Row 17 Ssk, k5, k2tog—7 sts.

Row 19 Ssk, k3, k2tog—5 sts.

Row 21 Ssk, k1, k2tog—3 sts.

Row 22 P3tog.

Fasten off.

Stem

Cast on 5 sts, and work in tube st until piece measures 11"/28cm.

Bind off.

Leaves

(make 2)

Cast on 5 sts.

Row 1 (RS) K2, yo, k1, yo, k2—7 sts.

Rows 2, 4, and 6 Purl.

Row 3 K3, yo, k1, yo, k3—9 sts.

Row 5 K4, yo, k1, yo, k4—11 sts.

Row 7 Bind off 3 sts, k1, yo, k1, yo, k5—10sts.

Row 8 Bind off 3 sts, p to end—7 sts.

Row 9 K3, yo, k1, yo, k3—9 sts.

Rows 10 and 12 Purl.

Row 11 K4, yo, k1, yo, k4—11 sts.

Row 13 As row 7.

Row 14 As row 8.

Row 15 Ssk, k3, k2tog—5 sts.

Rows 16 and 18 Purl.

Row 17 Ssk, k1, k2tog—3 sts.

Row 19 Sk2p.

Fasten off.

Coil bobble strip into a spiral to form sunflower center. Sew bobble strip, petals, leaves, and stem tube onto square as shown in photo.

SQUARE 8

Right panel

Cast on 48 sts, and work in stockinette st until piece measures 14"/35.5cm.

Bind off.

Left panel

Cast on 25 sts.

Row 1 and all odd rows (WS) K6, p4, k5, p4, k6.

Row 2 P6, 4-st RC, p5, 4-st RC, p6.

Rows 4, 6, and 8 P6, k4, p5, k4, p6.

Row 10 P6, 4-st LC, p5, 4-st LC, p6.

Rows 12, 14, and 16 As row 4.

Rep rows 1-16 until piece measures 14"/35.5cm, ending on a row 1 or 9. Bind off.

Flower

Work the same as flower in square 6.

Stem

Create a 4-st I-cord 12"/30.5cm long.

Leaves

(make 2)

Cast on 5 sts.

Row 1 (RS) K2, yo, k1, yo, k2—7 sts.

Even rows 2–12 Purl.

Row 3 K3, yo, k1, yo, k3—9 sts.

Row 5 K4, yo, k1, yo, k4—11 sts.

Row 7 Ssk, k7, k2tog—9 sts.

Row 9 Ssk, k5, k2tog—7 sts.

Row 11 Ssk, k3, k2tog—5 sts.

Row 13 Ssk, k1, k2tog—3 sts.

Row 14 P3tog.

Fasten off.

Sew panels together. Using 2 strands of yarn held together, work in whip st over seam.

Sew flower, stem, and leaves onto square as shown in photo.

Using 2 strands of yarn held together, work in stem st for swirls along side of stem.

SQUARE 9

Cast on 63 sts.

Rows 1–11 Knit.

Row 12 K9, p to last 9 sts, k9.

Row 13 Knit.

Rep rows 12 and 13 until piece measures 12"/30.5cm, then knit 11 rows.

Bind off.

Oak leaves

(make 3)

Cast on 7 sts.

Row 1 (RS) K3, yo, k1, yo, k3—9 sts.

Rows 2, 4, and 6 Purl.

Row 3 K4, yo, k1, yo, k4—11 sts.

Row 5 K5, yo, k1, yo, k5—13 sts.

Row 7 Bind off 3 sts, k1, yo, k1, yo, k7—12sts.

Row 8 Bind off 3 sts, p to end—9 sts.

Row 9 K4, yo, k1, yo, k4—11 sts.

Rows 10 and 12 Purl.

Row 11 K5, yo, k1, yo, k5—13 sts.

Row 13 As row 7.

Row 14 As row 8.

Row 15 Ssk, k5, k2tog—7 sts.

Rows 16, 18 and 20 Purl.

Row 17 Ssk, k3, k2tog—5 sts.

Row 19 Ssk, k1, k2tog—3 sts.

Row 21 Sk2p.

Fasten off.

Acorns

(make 3)

Cast on 10 sts.

Rows 1-11 Work in stockinette st.

Row 12 P2, * m1, p1; rep from * to end—18 sts.

Rows 13-18 Knit.

Row 19 K2tog 9 times—9 sts.

Row 20 K1, k2tog 4 times—5 sts.

Bind off.

Gather top and bottom of acorn, and stuff with small amounts of yarn.

Sew side seam.

Crochet a chain 3"/7.5cm to attach acorn to afghan.

Sew oak leaves and acorns onto square as shown in photo.

SQUARE 10

Cast on 60 sts, and work in stockinette st until piece measures 4½"/11.5cm, ending on a WS row.

Next 15 rows:

Row 1 (RS) K to last st, p1.

Row 2 K2, p to end.

Row 3 K to last 3 sts, p3.

Row 4 K4, p to end.

Row 5, 7, and 9 K to last 5 sts, p5.

Rows 6, 8, and 10 K5, p to end.

Row 11 K to last 11 sts, p1, k5, p5.

Row 12 K5, p5, k2, p to end.

Row 13 K to last 13 sts, p3, k5, p5.

Row 14 K5, p5, k4, p to end.

Row 15 K to last 15 sts, p5, k5, p5.

Cont as est, adding 1 more st to k5, p5 rib pat on each row, until all sts are in k5, p5 rib.

Work in k5, p5 rib pat until piece measures 14"/35.5cm.

Bind off.

Small patch

Cast on 19 sts, and work in garter st until piece measures 4½"/11.5cm.

Bind off.

Large patch

Cast on 30 sts.

Row 1 (RS) Knit.

Row 2 K1, p to last st, k1.

Rep rows 1 and 2 until piece measures 6"/15.25cm. Bind off.

Work 5 lazy daisies as shown in photo.

Work French knots at center of lazy daisies.

Work in whip st over diagonal line on main square where patterns switch.

Sew patches onto square as shown in photo.

Work uneven straight sts over borders of patches.

SQUARE 11

Cast on 62 sts, and work in stockinette st until piece measures 14"/35.5cm.

Bind off.

V and W letter shapes

Create 2 4-st I-cords 4"/10cm long, and curl into letter shapes.

Patch

Cast on 30 sts, and work in reverse stockinette st until piece measures 6"/15.25cm.

Bind off.

Work in Jacobean couching across patch as shown in photo.

Attach 1¼"/3cm fringes around border of patch.

Sew patch and letter shapes onto square as shown in photo.

Work in straight st for stems, and French knots for buds.

SQUARE 12

Cast on 59 sts, and work in seed st until piece measures 14"/35.5cm.

Bind off.

Small patch

Cast on 27 sts.

Row 1 K3, * p3, k3; rep from * to end.

Row 2 P3, * k3, p3; rep from * to end.

Rep rows 1 and 2 until piece measures 4½"/11.5cm.

Bind off.

Work 1 round in sc around border of patch.

Next rnd * (Sc, hdc, sc) into next st, skip 1 st, sc into next st, skip 1 st; rep from * around, sl st to connect.

Fasten off.

Large patch

Cast on 35 sts.

Rows 1 and 3 (RS) K1, * p3, k3; rep from * to last 4 sts, p3, k1.

Rows 2 and 4 P1, * k3, p3, rep from * to last 4 sts, k3, p1.

Rows 5 and 7 As row 2.

Rows 6 and 8 As row 1.

Rep rows 1–8 until piece measures 6"/15.25cm.

Bind off.

Attach 1¼"/3cm fringes around border of patch.

Sew patches onto square as shown in photo.

FINISHING

Assembly Sew squares together as shown in photo.

Using 2 strands of yarn held together, work in cross st over seams.

Border With RS facing, pick up and k 168 sts across top edge.

Working in garter st, inc 1 st at each end of needle every other row 6 times—180 sts.

Bind off.

Work bottom edge the same.

With RS facing, pick up and k 224 sts along one side edge, and work same as top border—236 sts.

Work other edge the same.

Sew corners together. Weave in all loose ends.

Snowflake Aran

An elegant combination of two knitting styles: six blocks each of a vibrant two-color intarsia snowflake and a bold Aran stitch pattern. They are sewn together to make the afghan and edged with a one-inch garter border. This is one you can knit while traveling!

54" x 72"/137cm x 183cm

MATERIALS
• 12 3½oz/100g skeins (each approx 132yd/120m) of Cascade Yarns *Pastaza* (50% llama, 50% wool) in #006 light gray (A)
• 6 skeins in #007 charcoal (B)
• 5 skeins in #049 red (C)
• Size U.S. 10 (6mm) needles OR SIZE TO OBTAIN GAUGE
• Cable needle
• Yarn needle

GAUGE
14 sts and 20 rows = 4"/10cm over stockinette st.
TAKE TIME TO CHECK GAUGE.

SPECIAL STITCHES
3-st PRC Sl 1 st to cn and hold to back, k2, p1 from cn.
3-st PLC Sl 2 st to cn and hold to front, p1, k2 from cn.
4-st RC Sl 2 sts to cn and hold to back, k2, k2 from cn.
4-st LC Sl 2 sts to cn and hold to front, k2, k2 from cn.
9-st LC Sl 5 sts to cn and hold to front, k4, sl 1 st back onto left needle from cn, p1, k4 from cn.
12-st RC Sl 8 sts to cn and hold to back, k4, sl 2nd 4 sts back onto left needle from cn, k4, k4 from cn.
12 st LC Sl 8 sts to cn and hold to front, k4, sl 2nd 4 sts back onto left needle from cn, k4, k4 from cn.
Make knot—(K1, p1) 3 times and k1 all into next st—7 sts, pass 2nd, 3rd, 4th, 5th, 6th and 7th sts over 1st—1 st.

REVERSE STOCKINETTE ST
All RS rows Purl.
All WS rows Knit.

WIDE CABLE PATTERN
(49 sts)
Row 1 (WS) (K2, p4) 4 times, k1, (p4, k2) 4 times.
Row 2 (P2, k4) 4 times, p1, (k4, p2) 4 times.
Row 3 As row 1.
Row 4 (P2, 4-st LC, p2, k4) twice, p1, (k4, p2, 4-st RC, p2) twice.
Row 5 As row 1.
Row 6 As row 2.
Row 7 As row 1.
Row 8 P2, 4-st LC, p2, k4, p2, 4-st LC, p2, 9-st LC, p2, 4-st RC, p2, k4, p2, 4-st RC, p2.
Row 9 As row 1.
Row 10 P2, k4, p2, * m1, (k4, p2) twice, k4, m1, p1; rep from * to last 7 sts, p1, k4, p2—53 sts.

Row 11 K2, p4, * k3, p4, (k2, p4) twice; rep from * to last 9 sts, k3, p4, k2.
Row 12 P2, 4-st LC, p3, m1, k4, p2tog, 4-st LC, p2tog, k4, m1, p3, m1, k4, p2tog, 4-st RC, p2tog, k4, m1, p3, 4-st RC, p2.
Row 13 K2, p4, k4, (p4, k1) twice, p4, k5, (p4, k1) twice, p4, k4, p4, k2.
Row 14 P2, k4, p4, m1, k3, skp, k4, k2tog, k3, m1, p5, m1, k3, skp, k4, k2tog, k3, m1, p4, k4, p2.
Row 15 K2, p4, k5, p12, k7, p12, k5, p4, k2.
Row 16 P2, 4-st LC, p5, m1, k4, 4-st LC, k4, m1, p7, m1, k4, 4-st RC, k4, m1, p5, 4-st RC, p2—57 sts.
Row 17 K2, p4, k6, p12, k9, p12, k6, p4, k2.
Row 18 P2, k4, p6, 12-st RC, p9, 12-st LC, p6, k4, p2.
Row 19 As row 17.
Row 20 P2, 4-st LC, p4, p2tog, k4, 4-st LC, k4, p2tog, p5, p2tog, k4, 4-st RC, k4, p2tog, p4, 4-st RC, p2—53 sts.
Row 21 As row 15.
Row 22 P2, k4, p3, * p2tog, (k4, m1) twice, k4, p2tog, p3; rep from * to last 6 sts, k4, p2.
Row 23 As row 13.
Row 24 P2, 4-st LC, p2, p2tog, k4, m1, p1, 4-st LC, p1, m1, k4, p2tog, p1, p2tog, k4, m1, p1, 4-st RC, p1, m1, k4, p2tog, p2, 4-st RC, p2.
Row 25 As row 11.
Row 26 P2, k4, p1, p2tog, (k4, p2) twice, k4, p3tog, (k4, p2) twice, k4, p2tog, p1, k4, p2—49 sts.
Row 27 As row 3.
Row 28 As row 8.
Rep rows 1–28 for wide cable pat.

NARROW CABLE PATTERN
(15 sts)
Row 1 (WS) K5, p5, k5.
Row 2 P5, k2, make knot, k2, p5.
Row 3 As row 1.
Row 4 P5, make knot, k3, make knot, p5.

Row 5 As row 1.

Row 6 As row 2.

Row 7 As row 1.

Row 8 P4, 3-st PRC, p1, 3-st PLC, p4.

Row 9 K4, p2, k1, p1, k1, p2, k4.

Row 10 P3, 3-st PRC, k1, p1, k1, 3-st PLC, p3.

Row 11 K3, p3, k1, p1, k1, p3, k3.

Row 12 P2, 3-st PRC, (p1, k1) twice, p1, 3-st PLC, p2.

Row 13 K2, p2, (k1, p1) 3 times, k1, p2, k2.

Row 14 P2, k3, (p1, k1) twice, p1, k3, p2.

Row 15 As row 13.

Row 16 P2, 3-st PLC, (p1, k1) twice, p1, 3-st PRC, p2.

Row 17 As row 11.

Row 18 P3, 3-st PLC, k1, p1, k1, 3-st PRC, p3.

Row 19 As row 9.

Row 20 P4, 3-st PLC, p1, 3-st PRC, p4.

Rep rows 1-20 for narrow cable pat.

ARAN SQUARES

(make 6)

Using A, cast on 85 sts.

Row 1 (WS) Work 3 sts in reverse stockinette st,

work 15 sts in narrow cable pat, work 49 sts in wide cable pat, work 15 sts in narrow cable pat, work 3 sts in reverse stockinette st.

Cont in est pats until piece measures 18"/45.5cm. Bind off.

SNOWFLAKE SQUARES

(make 6)

Using C, cast on 29 sts. Using B, cast on 29 more sts—58 sts.

Work snowflake chart in stockinette st, beg with a RS row.

Bind off in est colors.

BOBBLES

(make 30)

Using A, cast on 1 st.

Row 1 Kfb twice and k1 in front all into next st—5 sts.

Row 2 Purl.

Row 3 Knit.

Row 4 Purl.

Row 5 Ssk, k1, k2tog—3 sts.

Row 6 P3tog—1 st.

Fasten off, leaving a long tail.

EMBROIDERY

Using A, work in duplicate st for a diagonal line on snowflake squares.

FINISHING

Assembly Sew bobbles onto snowflake squares in center and at ends of diagonal gray lines.

Sew squares together, 3 wide and 4 long, alternating snowflake and aran squares.

Border Using B and with RS facing, pick up and k 188 sts across top edge.

Work in garter st for 5 rows, increasing 1 st at each end of needle every RS row twice—192 sts. Bind off.

Work bottom edge the same.

Using B and with RS facing, pick up and k 264 sts along one side edge, and work same as top border—268 sts.

Work other side edge the same.

Sew corners together. Weave in all loose ends.

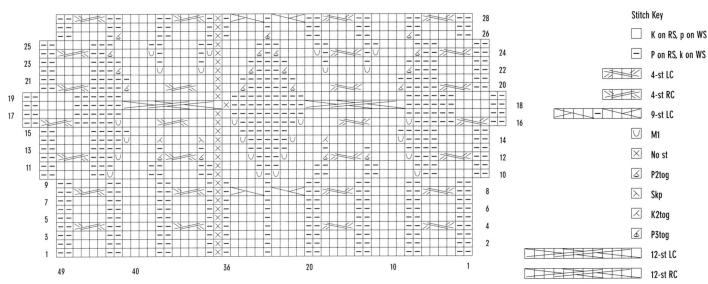

WIDE CABLE PATTERN

Stitch Key

☐ K on RS, p on WS

— P on RS, k on WS

4-st LC

4-st RC

9-st LC

⊔ M1

☒ No st

P2tog

Skp

K2tog

P3tog

12-st LC

12-st RC

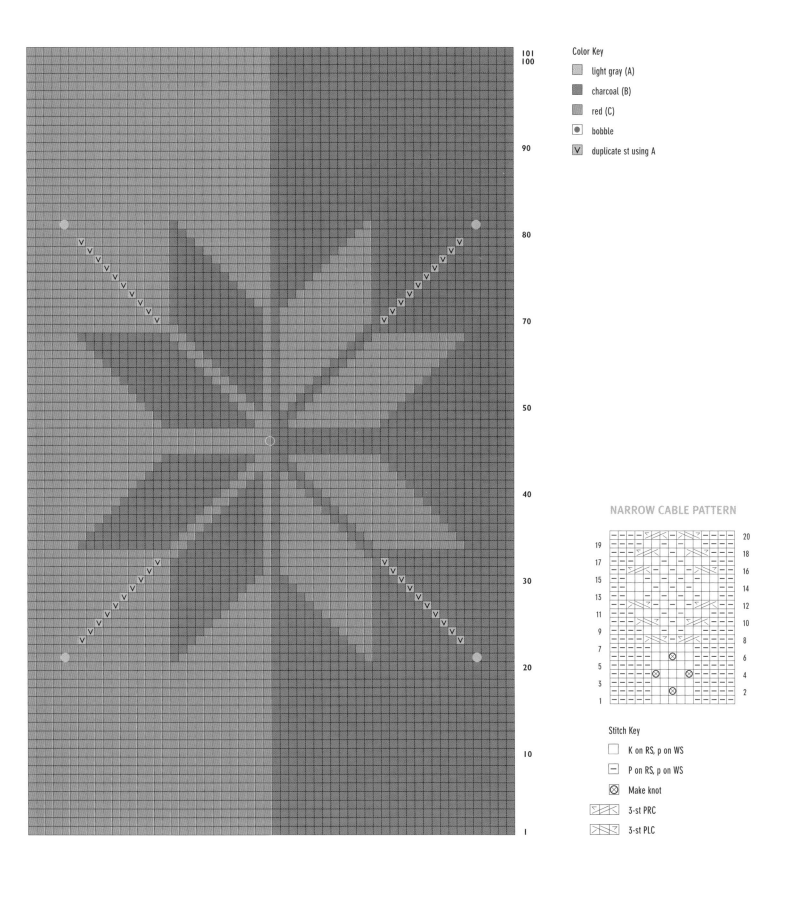

101
100

90

80

70

50

40

30

20

10

1

Color Key

light gray (A)

charcoal (B)

red (C)

⬤ bobble

V duplicate st using A

NARROW CABLE PATTERN

19 17 15 13 11 9 7 5 3 1
20 18 16 14 12 10 8 6 4 2

Stitch Key

☐ K on RS, p on WS

— P on RS, p on WS

⊗ Make knot

3-st PRC

3-st PLC

Diamond Lace

The afghan is worked in cotton, alternating a lace pattern stitch with an eyelet pattern. The eyelets are woven with satin ribbon; the solid diamonds have a daisy stitch embroidered in each center. The unique point edging is an unraveled fringe; the fringe is actually knit into the edging and then unraveled to create a finished effect.

52" x 66"/132cm x 168cm not including
edging

MATERIALS
• 26 1¾oz/50g skeins (each approx
108yd/99m) of Tahki Yarns/Tahki•Stacy
Charles, Inc. *Cotton Classic* (100%
cotton) in #3752 light green (A)
• 1 skein each in #3934 light purple
(B), #3942 dark purple (C),
#3534 yellow (D), and #3754 sage
green (E)
• Size U.S. 5 (3.75mm) circular needle
(used as a straight needle),
at least 36" length OR SIZE TO OBTAIN
GAUGE • 80 yds purple ribbon, approx
¼" in width
• Yarn needle

GAUGE
45 sts = 8½"/21.5cm over diamond
lace pat.
TAKE TIME TO CHECK GAUGE.

EYELET PATTERN
(10 sts)
Row 1 (RS) K1, k2tog, yo, k4, yo, ssk, k1.
Row 2 Purl, including yo's.
Rep rows 1 and 2 for eyelet pat.

DIAMOND LACE PATTERN
(45 sts)
Row 1 (RS) K1, (yo, ssk) twice, k2, * yo, ssk, yo, k3tog, yo, k1; * rep from * once more, k1, rep from * to * once more, k1, rep from * to * twice more, k1, (k2tog, yo) twice, k1.
Row 2 and all WS rows Purl, including yo's.
Row 3 K2, (yo, ssk) twice, k2, * yo, sk2p, yo, k3; * rep from * once more, k1, rep from * to * once more, k1, rep from * to * once more, yo, sk2p, yo, k2, (k2tog, yo) twice, k2.
Row 5 K3, (yo, ssk) twice, *k3, yo, ssk, yo, sk2p, yo, k3*; (k2tog, yo) twice, k1, (yo, ssk) twice, rep from * to * once more, (k2tog, yo) twice, k3.
Row 7 K4, (yo, ssk) twice, *k3, yo, sk2p, yo, k3*; (k2tog, yo) twice, k3, (yo, ssk) twice, rep from * to * once more, (k2tog, yo) twice, k4.
Row 9 * K5, (yo, ssk) twice, k7, (k2tog, yo) twice; rep from * once more, k5.
Row 11 K6, (yo, ssk) twice, k5, (k2tog, yo) twice, k7, (yo, ssk) twice, k5, (k2tog, yo) twice, k6.
Row 13 K7, (yo, ssk) twice, k3, (k2tog, yo) twice, k9, (yo, ssk) twice, k3, (k2tog, yo) twice, k7.
Row 15 K8, (yo, ssk) twice, k1, (k2tog, yo) twice, k11, (yo, ssk) twice, k1, (k2tog, yo) twice, k8.
Row 17 * K9, yo, ssk, yo, sk2p, yo, k2tog, yo, k4; rep from * once more, k5.
Row 19 * K10, k2tog, yo, k1, yo, ssk, k5; rep from * once more, k5.
Row 21 * K9, k2tog, yo, k3, yo, ssk, k4; rep from * once more, k5.
Row 23 * K10, yo, ssk, yo, k3tog, yo, k5; rep from * once more, k5.
Row 25 * K11, yo, sk2p, yo, k6; rep from * once more, k5.
Row 27 * K8, (k2tog, yo) twice, k1, (yo, ssk) twice, k3; rep from * once more, k5.
Row 29 * K7, (k2tog, yo) twice, k3, (yo, ssk) twice, k2; rep from * once more, k5.
Row 31 * K6, (k2tog, yo) twice, k5, (yo, ssk) twice, k1; rep from * once more, k5.
Row 33 * K5, (k2tog, yo) twice, k7, (yo, ssk) twice, rep from * once more, k5.
Row 35 K1, * k3, (k2tog, yo) twice, k9, (yo, ssk) twice; rep from * once more, k4.
Row 37 K2, * k1, (k2tog, yo) twice, k3, k2tog, yo, k1, yo, ssk, k3, (yo, ssk) twice, rep from * once more, k3.
Row 39 K2, (k2tog, yo) twice, *k3, k2tog, yo, k3, yo, ssk, k3*, yo, ssk, yo, sk2p, yo, k2tog, yo; rep from * to * once more, (yo, ssk) twice, k2.
Row 41 K1, (k2tog, yo) twice, k2, k2tog, yo, k1, yo, ssk, yo, k3tog, yo, k1, yo, k3, k3tog, yo, k1, yo, sk2p, k3, yo, k1, yo, ssk, yo, k3tog, yo, k1, yo, ssk, k2, (yo, ssk) twice, k1.
Row 43 K1, ssk, yo, k3, k2tog, yo, k3, yo, sk2p, yo, k3, yo, k1, k3tog, yo, k3, yo, sk2p, k1, yo, k3, yo, sk2p, yo, k3, yo, ssk, k3, yo, k2tog, k1.
Row 44 Purl.
Rep rows 1–44 for diamond lace pat.

Using A, cast on 287 sts.

Row 1 (RS) K1 (selvage), * work 10 sts in eyelet pat, work 45 sts in diamond lace pat; rep from * 4 more times, work 10 sts in eyelet pat, k1 (selvage).

Cont in pats as established until diamond lace pat has been worked 11 times.

Piece should measure approx 66"/168cm from beg.

Bind off.

EMBROIDERY

Embroider a flower in the center of each solid stockinette st diamond as follows:

Center Work a French knot using D for center of flower.

Petals Work petals in lazy daisy st using B or C alternately.

Work in straight st inside petals lengthwise using other shade of purple.

Leaves Work in straight st between petals, from the center out, using E.

FINISHING

Border Note: Sl all sts knitwise.

Using A, cast on 12 sts.

Row 1 (RS) Sl1, k11.
Row 2 K7, yo, k1, (yo, k2tog) twice—13 sts.
Row 3 Sl1, k3, p1, k8.
Row 4 K7, yo, k2, (yo, k2tog) twice—14 sts.
Row 5 Sl1, k3, p2, k8.
Row 6 K7, yo, k3 (yo, k2tog) twice—15 sts.
Row 7 Sl1, k3, p3, k8.
Row 8 K7, yo, k4, (yo, k2tog) twice—16 sts.
Row 9 Sl1, k3, p4, k8.
Row 10 K7, yo, k5 (yo, k2tog) twice—17 sts.
Row 11 Sl1, k3, p5, k8.
Row 12 K7, yo, k6, (yo, k2tog) twice—18 sts.
Row 13 Sl1, k3, p6, k8.
Row 14 K7, yo, k7, (yo, k2tog) twice—19 sts.
Row 15 Sl1, k3, p7, k8.
Row 16 K7, yo, k8 (yo, k2tog) twice—20 sts.
Row 17 Sl1, k3, p8, k8.
Row 18 K7, yo, k2tog, k7 (yo, k2tog) twice.
Row 19 Sl1, k3, p6, p2tog, k8—19 sts.
Row 20 K7, yo, k2tog, k6, (yo, k2tog) twice.
Row 21 Sl1, k3, p5, p2tog, k8—18 sts.
Row 22 K7, yo, k2tog, k5, (yo, k2tog) twice.
Row 23 Sl1, k3, p4, p2tog, k8—17 sts.
Row 24 K7, yo, k2tog, k4, (yo, k2tog) twice.
Row 25 Sl1, k3, p3, p2tog, k8—16 sts.
Row 26 K7, yo, k2tog, k3, (yo, k2tog) twice.
Row 27 Sl1, k3, p2, p2tog, k8—15 sts.
Row 28 K7, yo, k2tog, k2, (yo, k2tog) twice.
Row 29 Sl1, k3, p1, p2tog, k8—14 sts.
Row 30 K7, k2tog, k1, (yo, k2tog) twice—13 sts.
Row 31 Sl1, k3, p2tog, k7—12 sts.
Row 32 K8, (yo, k2tog) twice.

Rep rows 1–32 until border piece measures same as bottom edge of afghan, ending on a RS row.

Next row Bind off first 6 sts. Cut yarn, and slide tail through last bound-off st. Slide rem sts off the needle. Unravel first 6 sts of every row to create fringe. Sew straight edge to bottom edge of afghan.

Work same for top edge.

Block piece lightly

Weave lengths of ribbon vertically through each column of eyelets, and horizontally once at each border.

Weave in all loose ends.

Diamond Drapes

This classic afghan is made with a heather wool and is worked in three vertical panels that are then sewn together. The stitch pattern is an unusual combination of seed stitch and a wrapped rib that forms the diamonds. The top and bottom are edged with ribbed, unraveled fringe that is sewn on.

KNITTED MEASUREMENTS

46" x 58"/117cm x 147cm not including edging

MATERIALS

- 15 3.5oz/100g skeins (each approx 200yd/110m) of Harrisville Designs *New England Knitters Highland* (100% wool) in #45 Pearl
- Size U.S. 8 (5mm) needles OR SIZE TO OBTAIN GAUGE

GAUGE

16 sts (2 reps) and 24 rows = 4"/10cm over moss st pat.
44 sts = 8½"/21.5cm over diamond pat.
TAKE TIME TO CHECK GAUGE.

SLIP ST RIB PATTERN

(12 sts)

Note: Sl all sts purlwise wyib.

Row 1 (RS) P2, (k1, sl1, k1, p2) twice.

Row 2 K2, (p3, k2) twice.

Rep rows 1 and 2 for slip st rib pat.

MOSS ST PATTERN

(8 sts)

Rows 1 and 2 (K1, p1) 4 times.

Rows 3 and 4 (P1, k1) 4 times.

Rep rows 1–4 for moss st pattern

DIAMOND PATTERN

(44 sts)

Note: Sl all sts purlwise wyib.

Row 1 (RS) (P2, k2) 3 times, p2, * (m1, p1) twice, p1, (k2, p2) 3 times; rep from * to end.

Row 2 (K2, p2) 3 times, k2, * (p1, k1) twice, k1, (p2, k2) 3 times; rep from * to end.

Row 3 (P2, k2) 3 times, p2, * m1, p1, k1, p1, m1, p2, (k2, p2) 3 times; rep from * to end.

Row 4 (K2, p2) 3 times, k2, * (p1, k1) twice, p1, k2, (p2, k2) 3 times; rep from * to end.

Row 5 (P2, k2) 3 times, p2, * m1, (p1, k1) twice, p1, m1, p2, (k2, p2) 3 times; rep from * to end.

Row 6 (K2, p2) 3 times, k2, * (p1, k1) 4 times, k1, (p2, k2) 3 times; rep from * to end.

Row 7 (P2, k2) 3 times, p2, * m1, (p1, k1) 3 times, p1, m1, p2, (k2, p2) 3 times; rep from * to end.

Row 8 (K2, p2) 3 times, k2, * (p1, k1) 5 times, k1, (p2, k2) 3 times; rep from * to end.

Row 9 (P2, k2) 3 times, p2, * m1, (p1, k1) 4 times, p1, m1, p2, (k2, p2) 3 times; rep from * to end.

Row 10 * K1, kfb, sl10, pass 1st of sl sts over other 9, k2, (p1, k1) 5 times, p1; rep from * to last 14 sts, k1, kfb, sl10, pass 1st of sl sts over other 9, k2.

Row 11 (P2, k2) 3 times, p2, * ssk, (p1, k1) 3 times, p1, k2tog, p2, (k2, p2) 3 times; rep from * to end.

Row 12 (K2, p2) 3 times, k2, * (p1, k1) 5 times, k1, (p2, k2) 3 times; rep from * to end.

Row 13 (P2, k2) 3 times, p2, * ssk, (p1, k1) twice, p1, k2tog, p2, (k2, p2) 3 times; rep from * to end.

Row 14 (K2, p2) 3 times, k2, * (p1, k1) 4 times, k1, (p2, k2) 3 times; rep from * to end.

Row 15 (P2, k2) 3 times, p2, * ssk, p1, k1, p1, k2tog, p2, (k2, p2) 3 times; rep from * to end.

Row 16 (K2, p2) 3 times, k2, * (p1, k1) 3 times, k1, (p2, k2) 3 times; rep from * to end.

Row 17 (P2, k2) 3 times, p2, * ssk, p1, k2tog, p2, (k2, p2) 3 times; rep from * to end.

Row 18 (K2, p2) 3 times, k2, * (p1, k1) twice, k1, (p2, k2) 3 times; rep from * to end.

Row 19 (P2, k2) 3 times, p2, * s2kp, p2, (k2, p2) 3 times; rep from * to end.

Row 20 (K2, p2) 3 times, k2, * p1, k2, (p2, k2) 3 times; rep from * to end.

Rep rows 1–20 for diamond pat

LEFT PANEL

Cast on 73 sts.

Row 1 (WS) K2, (p3, k2) twice, (k1, p1) 4 times, (k2, p2) 3 times, k2, * p1, k2, (p2, k2) 3 times; rep from * once more, (k1, p1) 4 times, p1 (selvage).

Row 2 (RS) K1 (selvage), work 8 sts in moss st pat, work 44 sts in diamond pat, work 8 sts in moss st pat, work 12 sts in sl st rib pat.

Cont in pats as established until piece measures approx 58"/147cm from beg, ending on row 20 of diamond pat.

Bind off.

CENTER PANEL

Cast on 86 sts.

Row 1 (WS) P1 (selvage) k2, (p3, k2) twice, (k1, p1) 4 times, (k2, p2) 3 times, k2, * p1, k2, (p2, k2) 3 times; rep from * once more, (k1, p1) 4 times, k2, (p3, k2) twice, p1 (selvage).

Row 2 (RS) K1 (selvage), work 12 sts in sl st rib pat, work 8 sts in moss st pat, work 44 sts in diamond pat, work 8 sts in moss st pat, work 12 sts in sl st rib pat, k1 (selvage).

Cont in pats as established until piece measures approx 58"/147cm from beg, ending on row 20 of diamond pat.

Bind off.

RIGHT PANEL

Cast on 73 sts.

Row 1 (WS) P1 (selvage st), (k1, p1) 4 times, (k2, p2) 3 times, k2, *p1, k2, (p2, k2) 3 times; rep from * once more, (k1, p1) 4 times, k2, (p3, k2) twice.

Row 2 (RS) Work 12 sts in sl st rib pat, work 8 sts in moss st pat, work 44 sts in diamond pat, work 8 sts in moss st pat, k1 (selvage).

Cont in pats as established until piece measures approx 58"/147cm from beg, ending on row 20 of diamond pat.

Bind off.

FINISHING

Assembly Block panels lightly and sew together.

Fringe border Note: Sl all sts purlwise wyib.

Cast on 18 sts.

Row 1 (WS) (K2, p3) twice, k8.

Row 2 P8, (k1, sl1, k1, p2) twice.

Rep rows 1 and 2 until border piece measures same as bottom edge of afghan, ending on a RS row.

Next row Bind off 9 sts. Cut yarn, and slide tail through last bound off st. Slide rem sts off the needle. Unravel first 8 sts of every row to create fringe. Cut fringe evenly. Sew straight edge to bottom edge of afghan.

Work same for top edge.

Wedgwood

The influence here was Wedgwood china—thus the white-on-blue coloring and

relief appliqués. All of the motifs are made using cord, leaves and bobbles—all easy

stitch patterns—that are sewn onto a stockinette-stitch background. This is an

afghan a beginning knitter can easily make.

KNITTED MEASUREMENTS

51" x 58"/129.5cm x 147.5cm

MATERIALS

• 28 1¾oz/50g balls (each approx 98yd/90m) of GGH/Muench Yarns *Samoa* (50% cotton, 50% acrylic) in #57 blue (A)
• 7 balls in #4 off-white (B)
• Size U.S. 6 (4mm) circular needle (used as a straight needle), at least 36"/91.5cm length OR SIZE TO OBTAIN GAUGE
• Set of double pointed needles in same size (for I-cords)
• Long straight pins
• Yarn needle

GAUGE

18 sts and 28 rows = 4"/10cm over stockinette st.
TAKE TIME TO CHECK GAUGE.

I-CORD

Cast on 3 (or more) sts.
*K3 (or more) sts. Do not turn work.
Slide sts to right end of needle.
Pull yarn to tighten. Rep from * for desired length.

MAIN PANEL

Using A, cast on 120 sts, and work in stockinette st for 29"/73.5cm.
Bind off.
Stockinette st border Using A, cast on 216 sts, and work 2 rows in stockinette st, beg with a RS row.
Next 2 rows:
Row 1 K1, ssk, k to last 3 sts, k2tog, k1.
Row 2 Purl.
Rep rows 1 and 2 47 more times—120 sts.
Next row * K1, p1; rep from * to end.
Bind off knitwise. Sew bound-off edge of piece to top edge of main panel.
Work bottom edge the same.
Using A, cast on 254 sts and work same as top border—158 sts. Bind off knitwise.
Sew bound-off edge of piece to side edge of main panel.
Work other side edge the same.
Sew corners together.

LEAVES

(make 24)
Using B, cast on 5 sts.
Row 1 (RS) K2, yo, k1, yo, k2—7 sts.
Row 2 and all even rows Purl.
Row 3 K3, yo, k1, yo, k3—9 sts.
Row 5 K4, yo, k1, yo, k4—11 sts.
Row 7 K5, yo, k1, yo, k5—13 sts.
Row 9 Ssk, k9, k2tog—11 sts.
Row 11 Ssk, k7, k2tog—9 sts.
Row 13 Ssk, k5, k2tog—7 sts.
Row 15 Ssk, k3, k2tog—5 sts.
Row 17 Ssk, k1, k2tog—3 sts.
Row 19 Sk2p.
Cut yarn, and slide tail through rem loop.

BOBBLES

(make 70)
Using B, cast on 1 st.
Row 1 (K1, p1, k1, p1, k1) all into same st—5 sts.
Row 2 Knit.
Row 3 Purl.
Row 4 Knit.
Row 5 Purl.
Row 6 K2tog, k1, k2tog—3 sts.
Row 7 Sl1, p2tog, psso—1 st.
Cut yarn, and slide tail through rem loop.

FLOWER VASE

Using B, create 5 3-st I-cords 3½"/9cm long.
Using B, create 4 4-st I-cords: 28"/71cm, 5"/12.5cm, 5½"/14cm, and 6"/15cm long.

STEMS

Using B, create 6 3-st I-cords: 2 8"/20.5cm long, 2 12"/30.5cm long, and 2 15"/38cm long.

CENTER CORD FRAMES

Straight frames Using B, create 2 4-st I-cords: 52"/132cm and 62"/157.5cm long.
Wavy frame Using B, create a 2-st I-cord 66"/168cm long.

OUTER EDGE CORD FRAMES

Straight frames Using B, create 2 4-st I-cords: 184"/467cm and 204"/518cm long.
Wavy frame Using B, create a 2-st I-cord 208"/528cm long.

BOWS

Using B, create 8 4-st I-cords: 4 14"/35.5cm long, and 4 2"/5cm long.

LARGE WAVE

Using B, create a 5-st I-cord 180"/457cm long.

FINISHING

Assembly Pin embellishments in place according to photo. Using B, sew pieces in place. Weave in all loose ends.

Mudcloth

This afghan is inspired in color and pattern by African mudcloths. Using two colors, it is worked in two large vertical panels that are sewn together at the center. The top- and bottom-edge fringes are cut and braided, adding to the character of the piece.

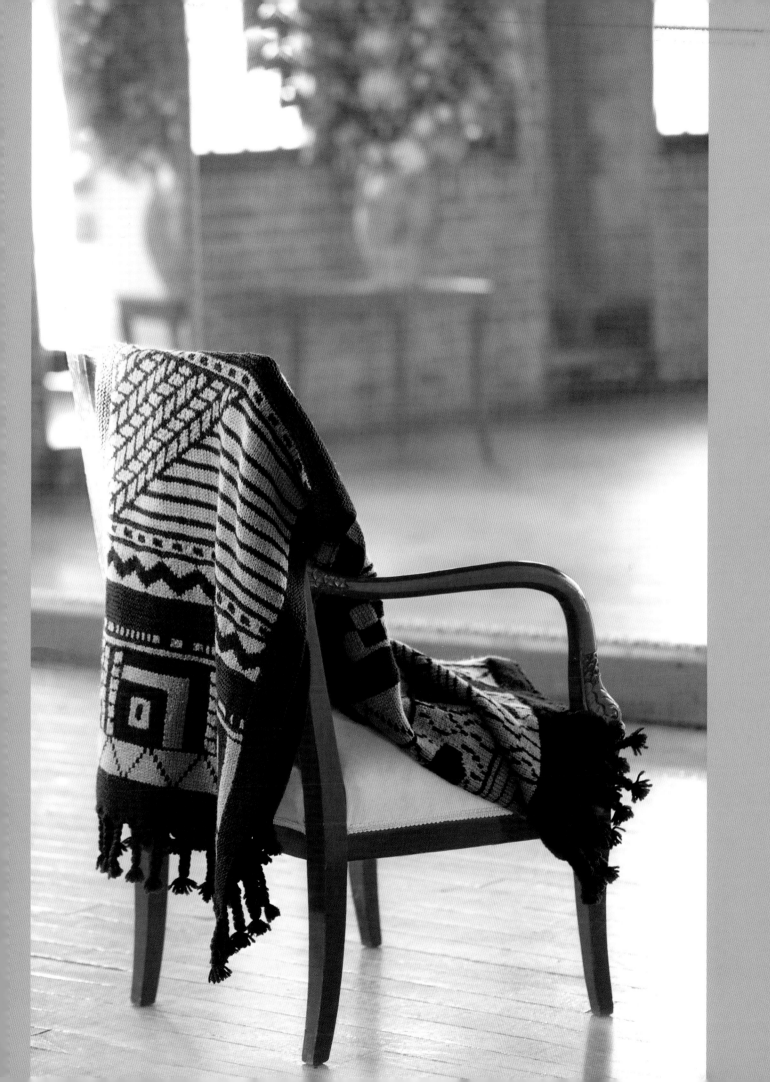

KNITTED MEASUREMENTS

46" x 64"/117cm x 162cm not including fringe

MATERIALS

• 9 3½oz/100g balls (each approx 210yd/193m) of Patons *Decor* (75% wool, 25% acrylic) in #1603 black (A)
• 7 balls in #1632 rich taupe (B)
• Size U.S. 8 (5mm) straight needles OR SIZE TO OBTAIN GAUGE
• Size U.S. 8 (5mm) circular needle (used as a straight needle), at least 36"/91.5cm long OR SIZE TO OBTAIN GAUGE

GAUGE

18 sts and 24 rows = 4"/10cm over stockinette st.
TAKE TIME TO CHECK GAUGE.

MAIN PANELS

(make 1 for each chart)
Using A, cast on 91 sts, and work in intarsia, working chart 1 for left panel and chart 2 for right panel.
Bind off.

CENTER CONNECTING PANEL

Using circular needle and A and with RS facing, pick up and k 270 sts evenly along left edge of right panel.
Work in garter st for 2"/5cm.
Bind off.

FINISHING

Assembly Sew left edge of center connecting panel to right edge of left panel.

Border Using A and with RS facing, pick up and k 191 sts along top edge.
Working in garter st, inc 1 st at each end of needle every RS row 8 times—207 sts.
Knit 1 more row, then bind off.
Work bottom edge the same.
Using A and with RS facing, pick up and k 270 sts along one side edge, and work same as top border until there are 286 sts. K 1 more row, then bind off.
Work other edge the same.
Sew corners together. Weave in all loose ends.
Fringe Attach 93 4½"/11.5cm 6-strand fringes in A evenly along top edge. Braid together sets of 3 fringes, and knot at bottom of braid to secure.

CHART 1 (START)

100
90
80
70
60
50
40
30
20
10
1

CHART 1 (CONTINUED)

Color Key

- 1603 (A)
- 1632 (B)
- P on RS rows, K on WS rows

CHART 1 (CONTINUED)

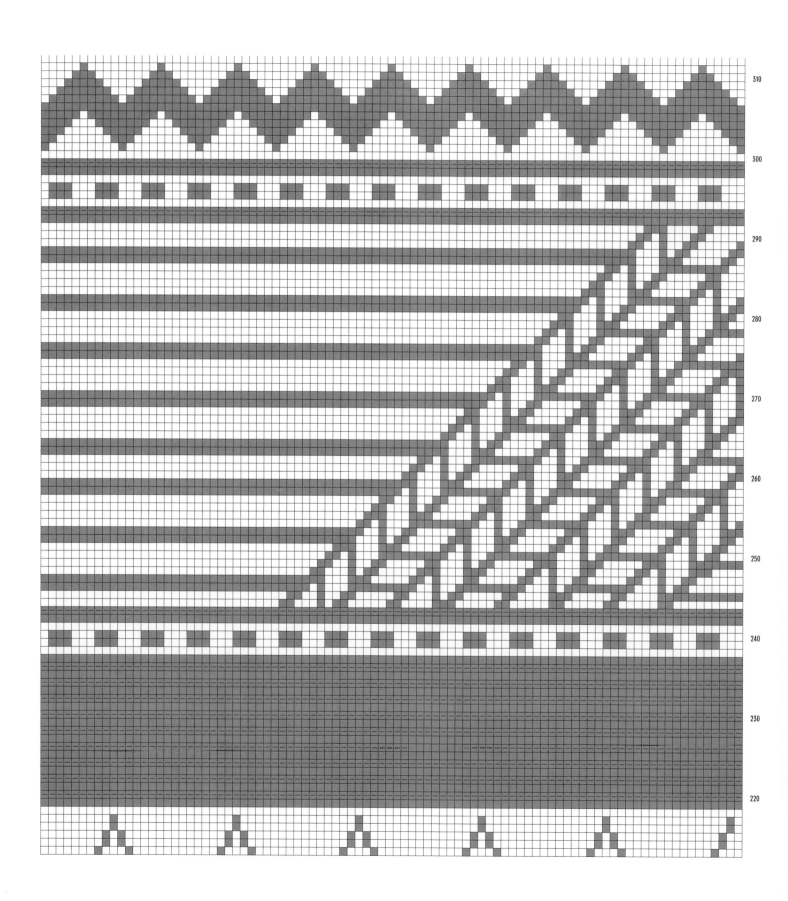

CHART 1 (END)

Color Key

1603 (A)

1632 (B)

P on RS rows, K on WS rows

CHART 2 (START)

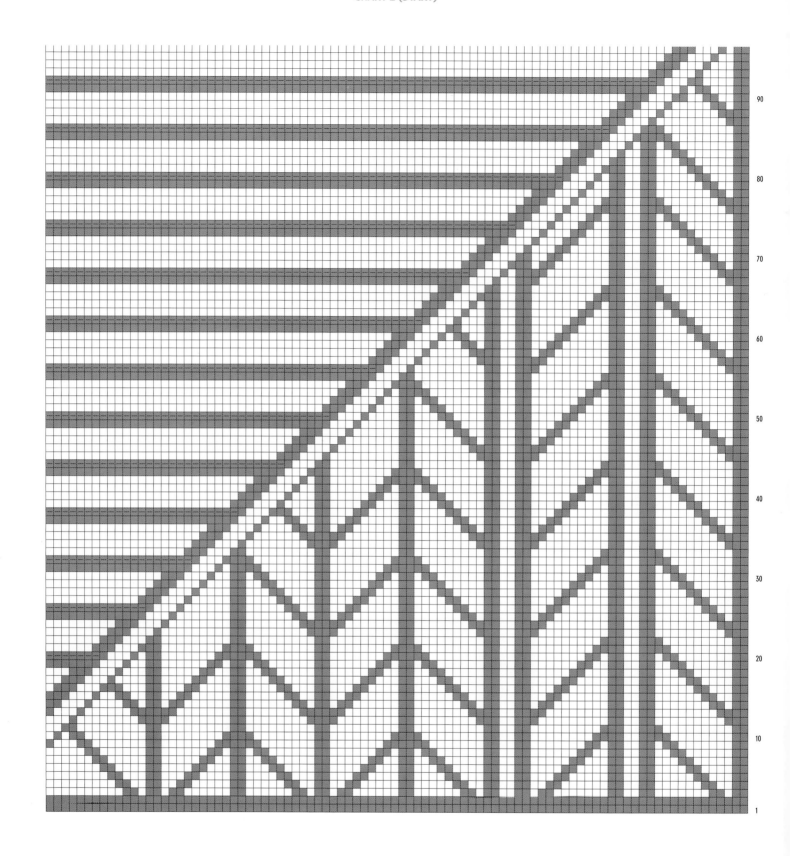

90

80

70

60

50

40

30

20

10

1

Color Key

 1603 (A)

☐ 1632 (B)

■ P on RS rows, K on WS rows

CHART 2 (CONTINUED)

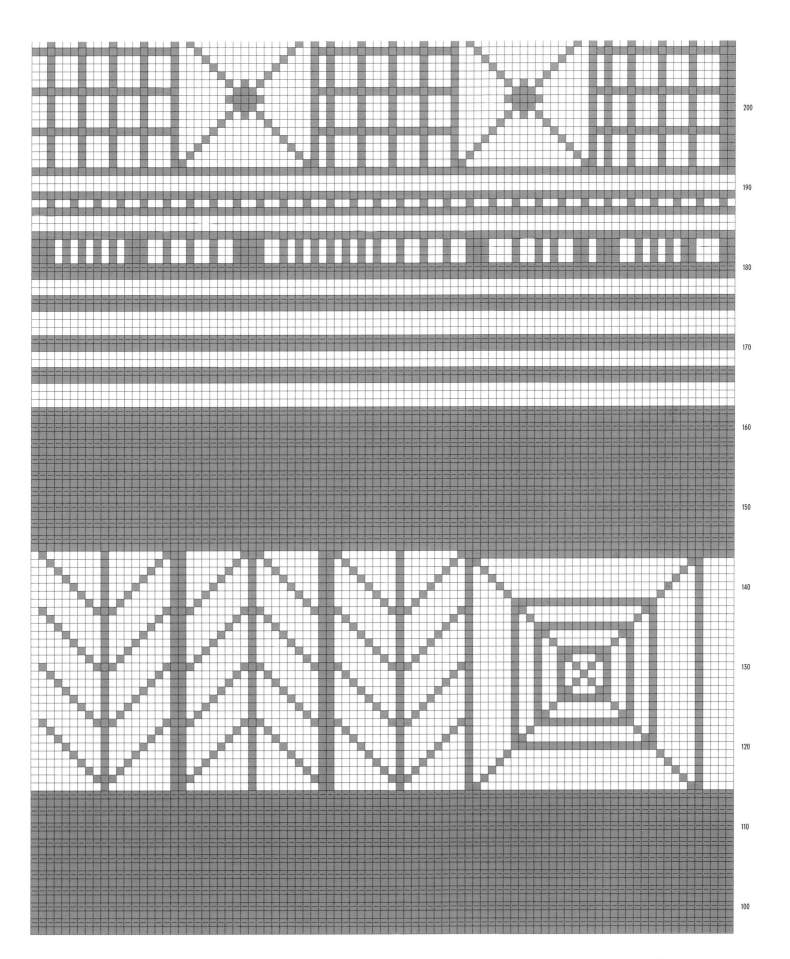

200

190

180

170

160

150

140

130

120

110

100

CHART 2 (CONTINUED)

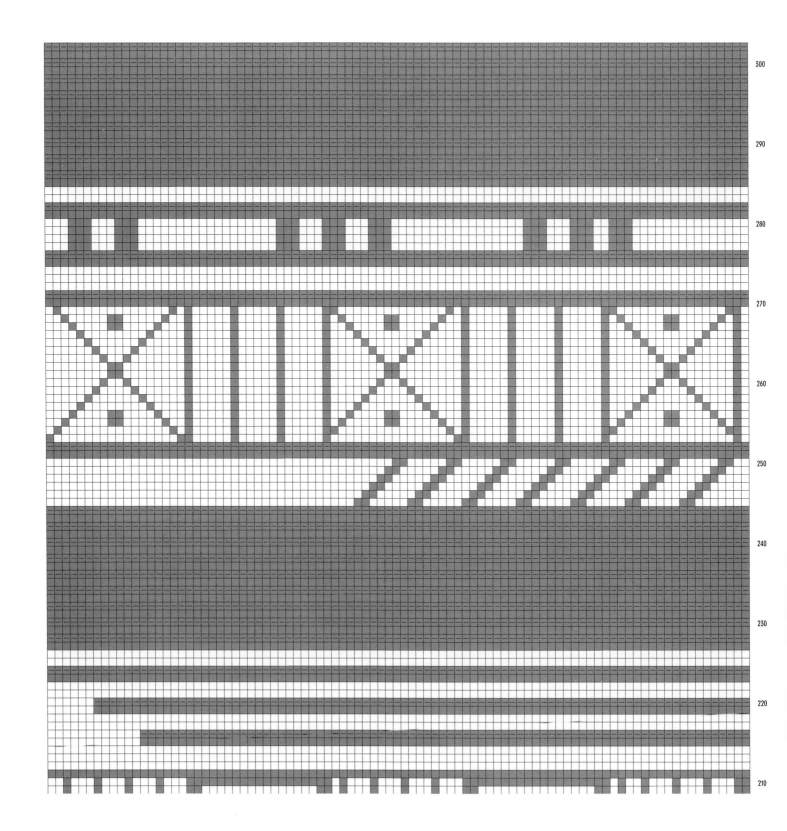

CHART 2 (END)

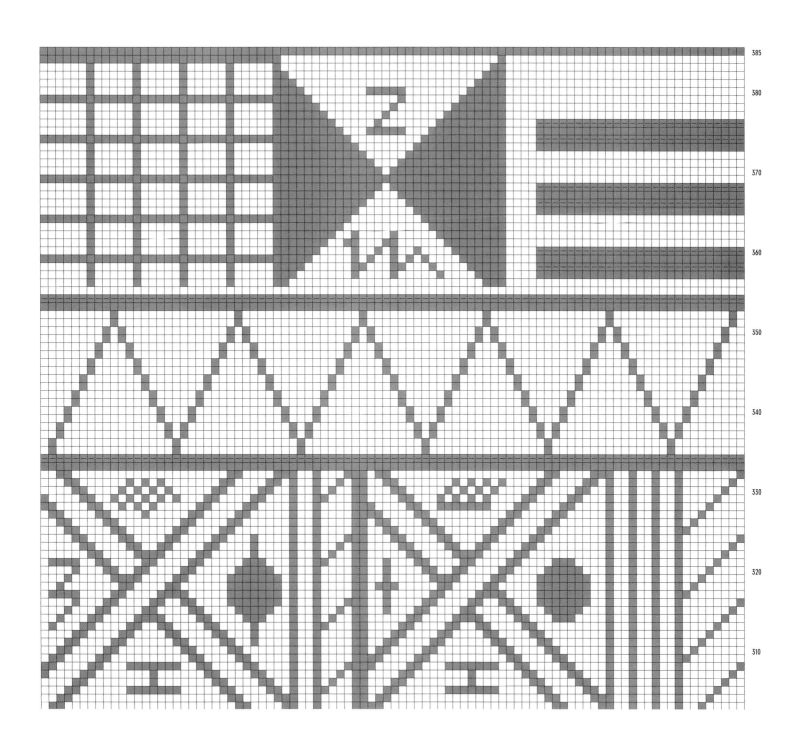

385
380
375
370
365
360
355
350
345
340
335
330
325
320
315
310

Color Key

 1603 (A)

☐ 1632 (B)

▨ P on RS rows, K on WS rows

Regal Tapestry

The inspiration for this afghan comes from a small part of a Persian rug that I own; I have used elements from the rug in many of my designs over the years. When doing an intarsia piece like this, you have to repeat some of the chart because of the limited printing space in a book or a magazine. The center chart will need to be mirrored as well as reversed, as will the top and side charts. I used a Fair Isle peerie border around the center and outer edges. The outer edge has a mitered folded edge. I applied bobbles for textural dimension.

45" x 60"/114cm x 151.5cm

MATERIALS

• 17 (1¾oz/50g) skeins (each approx 137 yd/125m) RYC/Westminster Fibers, Inc., *Pure Wool DK* (100% superwash wool) in #009 Ultramarine (A)
• 1 skein each in #032 Gilt (B), #014 Hay (C), #033 Honey (D), #015 Barley (E), #016 Hessian (F), #019 Avocado (G), #021 Glade (H), #022 Emerald (I), #023 Shamrock (J), #020 Parsley (K), #005 Glacier (L), #006 Pier (M), #007 Cypress (N), #008 Marine (O), #039 Lavender (P), #036 Kiss (Q), #034 Spice (R), #028 Raspberry (S), #029 Pomegranate (T), #040 Tangerine (U), #035 Quarry (V) and #013 Enamel (W)
• Size U.S. 7 (4.5mm) circular needle (used as a straight needle), at least 36"/91.5cm length OR SIZE TO OBTAIN GAUGE
• Yarn needle

GAUGE

20 sts and 26 rows = 4"/10cm over stockinette st.
TAKE TIME TO CHECK GAUGE.

CENTER PANEL

Using A, cast on 141 sts, and work chart 1 through row 148.
Turn chart upside down, and work it in reverse from row 148 to row 1.
Bind off.

TOP AND BOTTOM BORDER

Using A and with RS facing, pick up and k 141 sts along top edge. Purl one row.
Next row (RS) Work chart 2, then work it again in reverse, being sure to knit center st only once. Cont as est until chart 2 is complete, increasing 1 st at each end of needle every other row—201 sts.
Using A, knit 2 rows for turning ridge.
Next 2 rows:
Row 1 (RS) K1, ssk, k to last 3 sts, k2tog, k1.
Row 2 Purl.
Rep rows 1 and 2 until hem measures 1½"/4cm.
Bind off. Work bottom edge the same.

SIDE BORDERS

Using A and with RS facing, pick up and k 221 sts along one side edge. Purl one row.
Next row (RS) Work chart 3, then work it again in reverse, being sure to knit center st only once. Cont as est until chart 3 is complete, increasing 1 st at each end of needle every other row—281 sts.
Work hem same as top and bottom border.
Bind off. Work other edge the same.

BOBBLES

(make 112 using P, 46 using L, 24 using Q, and 16 using N)
Cast on 1 st.
Row 1 Kfb twice and k1 all into next st—5 sts.
Row 2 Purl.
Row 3 Knit.
Row 4 Purl.
Row 5 Pass 2nd, 3rd, 4th, and 5th sts over 1st—1 st.
Fasten off.

EMBROIDERY

Flower petals and berries on border Using Q or S as indicated, work French knots.
Leopard spots Using W, work French knots,
Butterfly details Using B, work short straight sts.
Stems Using G, K, U, or W as indicated, work stem st.

FINISHING

Assembly Sew border pieces to center panel. Sew corners together. Sew down bobbles as indicated by chart. Fold hems to WS and sew down. Weave in all loose ends.

CHART 1

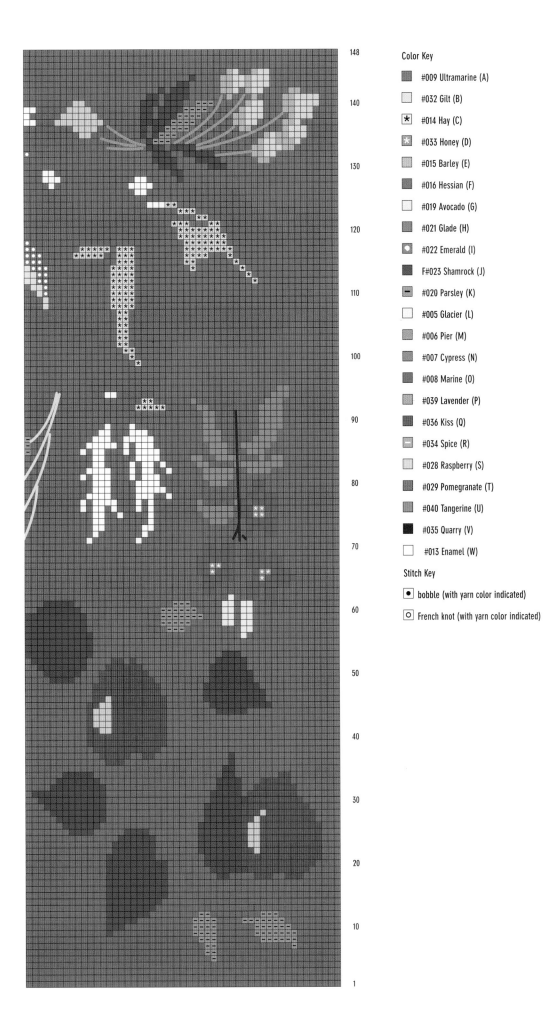

148

140

130

120

110

100

90

80

70

60

50

40

30

20

10

1

Color Key

▩	#009 Ultramarine (A)
▢	#032 Gilt (B)
✱	#014 Hay (C)
✳	#033 Honey (D)
▩	#015 Barley (E)
▩	#016 Hessian (F)
▢	#019 Avocado (G)
▩	#021 Glade (H)
◉	#022 Emerald (I)
▩	F#023 Shamrock (J)
⊟	#020 Parsley (K)
▢	#005 Glacier (L)
▩	#006 Pier (M)
▩	#007 Cypress (N)
▩	#008 Marine (O)
▩	#039 Lavender (P)
▩	#036 Kiss (Q)
▭	#034 Spice (R)
▩	#028 Raspberry (S)
▩	#029 Pomegranate (T)
▩	#040 Tangerine (U)
▩	#035 Quarry (V)
▢	#013 Enamel (W)

Stitch Key

⊡	bobble (with yarn color indicated)
⊙	French knot (with yarn color indicated)

CHART 2 TOP AND BOTTOM BORDERS

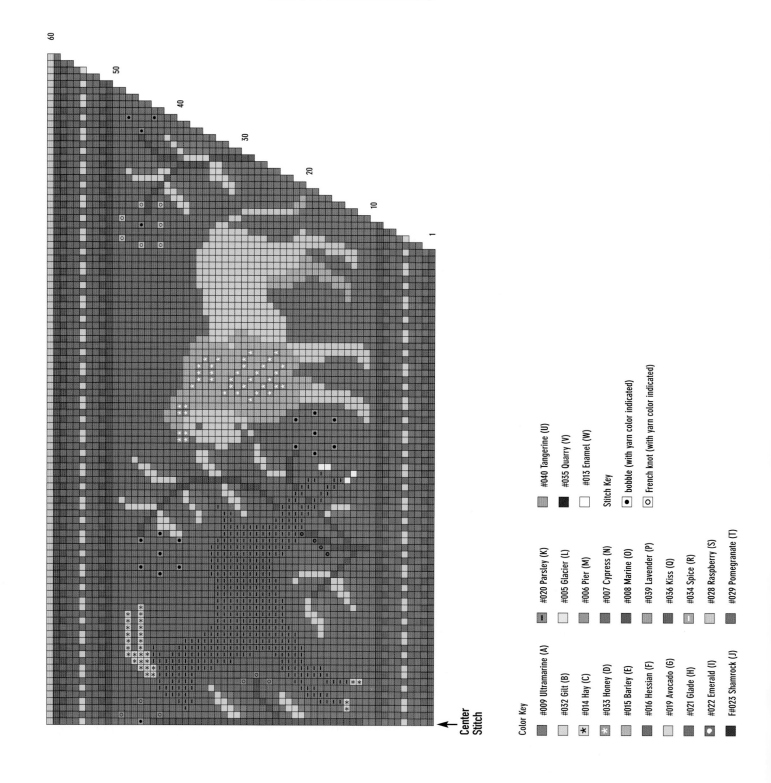

Center Stitch

Color Key

#009 Ultramarine (A)
#052 Gilt (B)
#014 Hay (C) ★
#033 Honey (D) ✳
#015 Barley (E)
#016 Hessian (F)
#019 Avocado (G)
#021 Glade (H)
#022 Emerald (I)
F#023 Shamrock (J)

#020 Parsley (K)
#005 Glacier (L)
#006 Pier (M)
#007 Cypress (N)
#008 Marine (O)
#039 Lavender (P)
#056 Kiss (Q)
#034 Spice (R)
#028 Raspberry (S)
#029 Pomegranate (T)

#040 Tangerine (U)
#035 Quarry (V)
#013 Enamel (W)

Stitch Key

● bobble (with yarn color indicated)
○ French knot (with yarn color indicated)

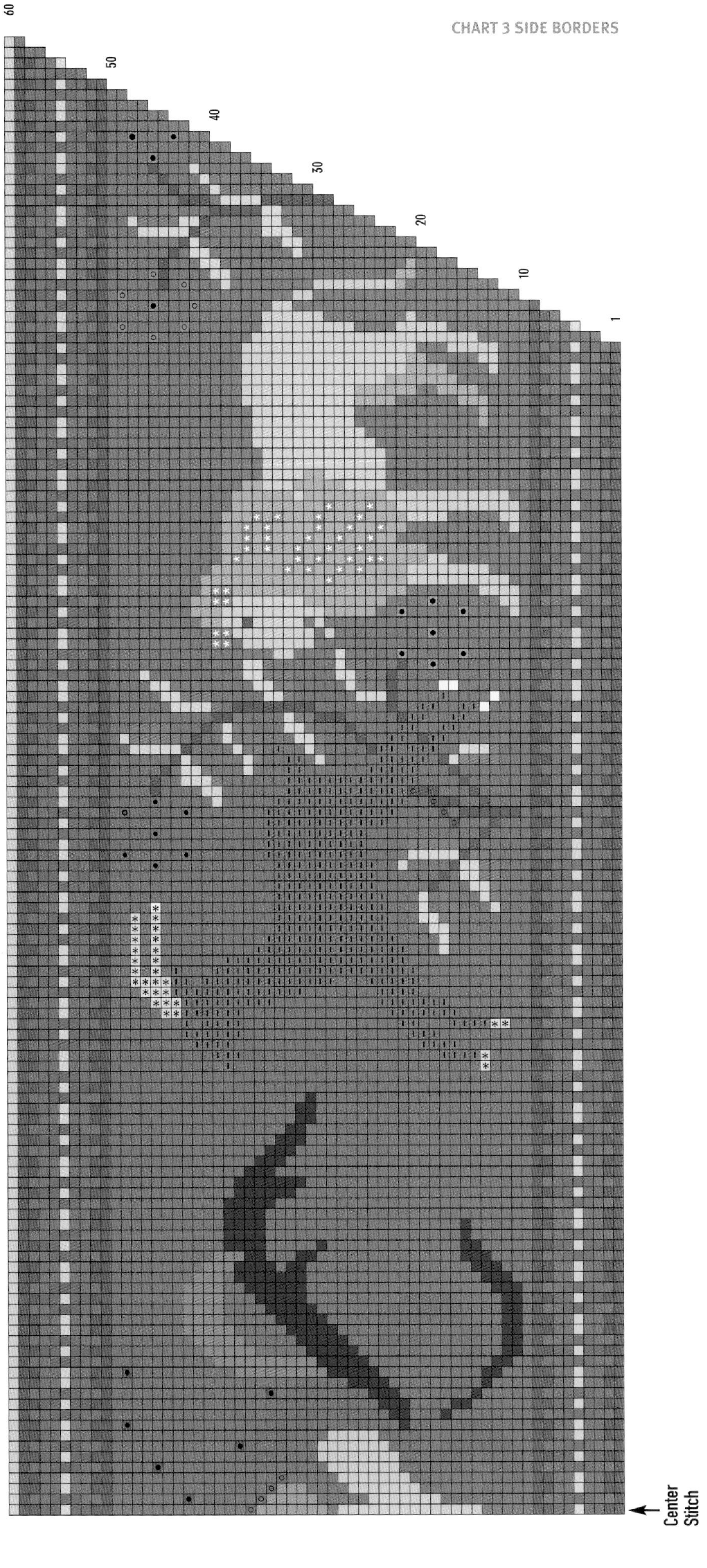

CHART 3 SIDE BORDERS

60

50

40

30

20

10

1

← Center
Stitch

Sun Visions

This afghan consists of 6 large blocks worked in stockinette stitch. A horseshoe cable pattern connects the blocks. Each sun is made unique by using a different edging for the sun's circumference. This is a major example of "thinking outside the box" in using different edgings. The pleasant faces are worked in duplicate stitch after the pieces are knit. The outer border is garter stitch with a color change. This delightful creation really brightens my sun room.

KNITTED MEASUREMENTS

Each square 21" x 21"/53.5cm x 53.5cm

Afghan 46" x 69"/117cm x 175cm

MATERIALS

- 12 3½oz/100g skeins (each approx 205yd/187m) of Classic Elite Yarns *Provence* (100% mercerized cotton) in #2616 Natural (A)
- 8 skeins in #2678 Portabello (B)
- 1 skein in #2661 Summer Wheat (C)
- Size U.S. 6 (4mm) needles OR SIZE TO OBTAIN GAUGE
- Size U.S. 6 (4mm) circular needle, 36"/90cm long
- Cable needle
- Stitch holders
- Yarn needle

GAUGE

20 sts and 26 rows = 4"/10cm over stockinette st.

TAKE TIME TO CHECK GAUGE.

SPECIAL STITCHES

4-st LC Sl 2 sts to cn and hold to front, k2, k2 from cn.

4-st RC Sl 2 sts to cn and hold to back, k2, k2 from cn.

Make bobble Kfb twice and k1 all into next st, (turn, p5, turn, k5) twice, pass 2nd, 3rd, 4th, and 5th sts over 1st.

I-CORD

Using dp needle, cast on 5 sts. *K5 sts. Do not turn work. Slide sts to right end of needle. Pull yarn to tighten. Rep from * for desired length.

SQUARES

(make 6)

Using A, cast on 105 sts, and work in stockinette st for 21"/53.5cm.

Bind off.

SUN RAY FRAME 1 (TOP LEFT)

Using B, cast on 13 sts.

Row 1 (WS) Sl1, p1, p2tog, yo, k9—13 sts.

Row 2 Sl1, k8, yo, k2, k1 tbl, k1—14 sts.

Row 3 Sl1, p2, yo, p2tog, yo, k9—15 sts.

Row 4 Sl1, k8, yo, k2tog, yo, k2, k1 tbl, k1—16 sts.

Row 5 Sl1, p2, (yo, p2tog) twice, yo, k9—17 sts.

Row 6 Sl1, k8, (yo, k2tog) twice, yo, k2, k1tbl, k1—18 sts.

Row 7 Sl1, p2, (yo, p2tog) 3 times, yo, k9—19 sts.

Row 8 Sl1, k8, (yo, k2tog) 3 times, yo, k2, k1 tbl, k1—20 sts.

Row 9 Sl1, p2, (yo, p2tog) 4 times, yo, k9—21 sts.

Row 10 Bind off 8 sts, k10, k1 tbl, k1—13 sts.

Rep rows 1–10 21 more times.

Bind off. Sew together bound-off and cast-on edges to form a circle.

SUN RAY FRAME 2

Using B, create a 5-st I-cord 11"/28cm long. Cut yarn, and place all sts on a st holder.

Make 6 more pieces the same, and 7 more pieces 8"/20.5cm in length.

Place all pieces back on the needle, in alternating lengths.

Next 3 rows

Row 1 Cast on 1 st (selvage), * k5, cast on 5 sts, rep from * 13 more times, cast on 1 st (selvage)—142 sts.

Row 2 P1, * k5, p5, rep from * 13 more times, p1.

Row 3 K1, * k5, p5, rep from * 13 more times, k1.

Rep rows 2 and 3 for 1"/2.5cm.

Bind off. Sew edges together to form circle.

SUN RAY FRAME 3

Using B, cast on 23 sts.

Rows 1 and 2 Knit.

Row 3 Bind off 19 sts, k to end.

Row 4 K4, cast on 19 sts using cable cast-on.

Rows 5 and 6 Knit.

Row 7 Bind off 19 sts, k to end.

Rep rows 4–7 until you have 51 spokes.

Bind off. Sew together bound-off and cast-on edges to form a circle.

SUN RAY FRAME 4

Bobbles Using B, cast on 1 st, and make bobble. Cut yarn, leaving a 24"/61cm tail, slide tail through rem loop.

Make 11 more bobbles the same.

Bobble Tube Note: Sl all sts purlwise.

Using B, cast on 5 sts.

Row 1 K1 (sl1, k1) twice.

Row 2 Sl1, (p1, sl1) twice.

Rep rows 1 and 2 3 more times.

Row 9 K1, sl1, make bobble, sl1, k1.

Row 10 As row 2.

Rep rows 1–10 35 more times.

Bind off. Sew together bound-off and cast-on edges to form a circle.

Sun rays Using B, cast on 2 sts.

Row 1 K2.

Row 2 Yo, k2.

Row 3 Yo, k3.

Cont in this manner until you have 18 sts. Cut yarn, leaving all sts on the needle.

Make 11 more rays the same.

Next row (WS) K8, (k2tog, k16) 11 times, k2tog, k8—204 sts.

Bind off. Sew edges together to form circle.

Sew bobble tube to inside of sun rays piece.

SUN RAY FRAME 5

Triple bobble Note: Sl all sts purlwise.

Using B, cast on 1 st.

* **Row 1 (RS)** Kfb twice and k1 all into same st—5 sts.

Row 2 Sl1, p4.

Row 3 Sl1, k4.

Row 4 Sl1, p4.

Rows 5-8 Rep rows 3 and 4 twice more.

Row 9 K2tog, k1, k2tog—3 sts.

Row 10 P3tog—1 st.

Turn work and fold bobble in half. Insert tip of left needle into cast-on st and k it tog with rem st of bobble. Rep from * twice more, leaving last st on the needle.

Sun ray Work from rem st of triple bobble.

Row 1 (RS) Kfb and k1 all into same st—3 sts.

Row 2 and all even rows Purl.

Row 3 K1, (yo, k1) twice—5 sts.

Row 5 K2, yo, k1, yo, k2—7 sts.

Row 7 K3, yo, k1, yo, k3—9 sts.

Row 9 K4, yo, k1, yo, k4—11 sts.

Row 11 K5, yo, k1, yo, k5—13 sts.

Row 13 K6, yo, k1, yo, k6—15 sts.

Row 15 K7, yo, k1, yo, k7—17 sts.

Cut yarn, leaving all sts on the needle.

Make 10 more pieces the same—187 sts.

Work in stockinette st across all sts for 3 rows, beg on a WS row.

Work in k1, p1 rib for 1"/2.5cm.

Bind off. Sew edges together to form circle.

SUN RAY FRAME 6

Note: Cross all loops in front when joining.

Using B, cast on 40 sts.

Row 1 (RS) K to last 3 sts, yo, k2tog, k1.

Row 2 Sl1, p to end.

Row 3 Bind off 28 sts (1 spoke made), k to last 3 sts, yo, k2tog, k1—12 sts.

Row 4 Sl1, k to end.

Row 5 K to last 3 sts, yo, k2tog, k1.

Row 6 Sl1, k2, p to end.

Row 7 As row 5.

Row 8 As row 4.

Row 9 As row 5.

Row 10 As row 6.

Row 11 As row 5.

Row 12 Sl1, k to end, cast on 28 sts using the cable cast-on—40 sts.

Row 13 As row 5.

Row 14 As row 6.

Row 15 Bind off 28 sts (1 spoke made), k to last 3 sts, yo, k2tog, k1—12 sts.

Row 16 As row 4.

Row 17 As row 5.

Row 18 As row 6.

Row 19 As row 5.

Row 20 Sl1, k10, turn up end of 1st spoke and k 1st bound-off st tog with last st on needle (1 loop made).

Row 21 As row 5.

Row 22 Sl 1, k2, p8, k other thread of same bound-off st tog with last st on needle.

Row 23 As row 5.

Row 24 As row 12.

Rep rows 13–24 21 more times.

Pick up and k 40 sts at cast-on edge. Using 3rd needle, join edges by working 3-needle bind-off. Tack down last spoke.

CABLE PANELS

Using A, cast on 14 sts.

Row 1 (RS) K1, p2, k8, p2, k1.

Row 2 and all even rows K the k sts, p the p sts.

Row 3 K1, p2, 4-st RC, 4-st LC, p2, k1.

SUN RAY 1

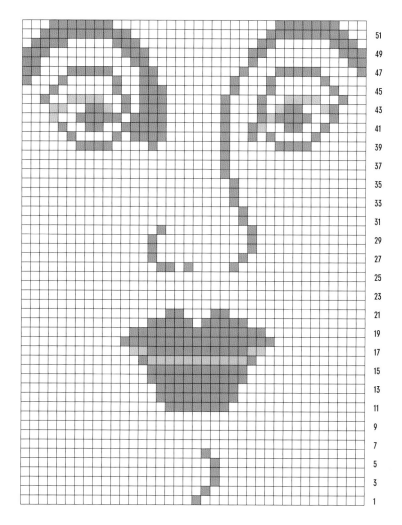

51
49
47
45
43
41
39
37
35
33
31
29
27
25
23
21
19
17
15
13
11
9
7
5
3
1

SUN RAY 2

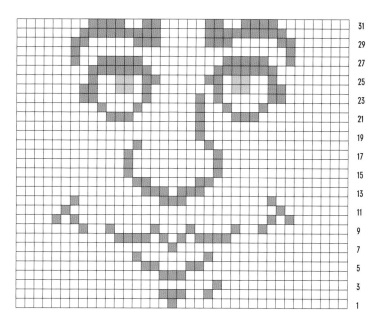

31
29
27
25
23
21
19
17
15
13
11
9
7
5
3
1

Color Key

☐ 2616 (A)

▨ 2678 (B)

▨ 2661 (C)

☐ center of design;
center of block

SUN RAY 3

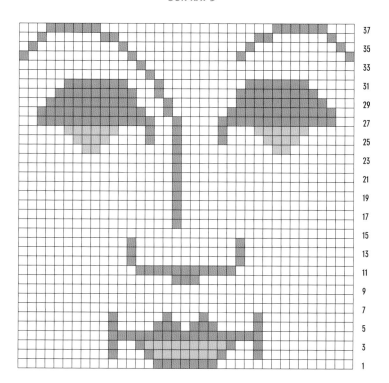

37
35
33
31
29
27
25
23
21
19
17
15
13
11
9
7
5
3
1

Row 5 As row 1.

Row 7 K1, p2, 4-st LC, 4-st RC, p2, k1.

Row 8 As row 2.

Rep rows 1–8 until piece measures 21"/53.5cm. Bind off.

Make 3 more pieces the same, and 1 more piece 67"/170cm in length.

EMBROIDERY

Work in duplicate st, working 1 face chart on each square.

FINISHING

Assembly Sew short cable panels horizontally between squares to make 2 panels of 3 squares each. Sew long cable panel vertically between square panels.

Use a bowl or plate to lay out sun ray frames around faces, and sew down.

Using B, embroider a long star in straight st at each point of sun ray frame #1.

Curl I-cords into spirals when sewing down sun ray frame #2.

Sew individual bobbles between rays of sun ray frame #4.

Border Using B and with RS facing and circular needle, pick up and k 208 sts across top of afghan, and knit 1 row.

Change to A.

Row 1 (RS) Kfb, k to last 2 sts, kfb, k1.

Row 2 Knit.

Rep rows 1 and 2 twice more.

Bind off.

Work bottom edge the same.

Using B and with RS facing and circular needle, pick up and k 372 sts along one side edge, and work same as top border.

Work other edge the same.

Sew corners together. Weave in all loose ends.

SUN RAY 4

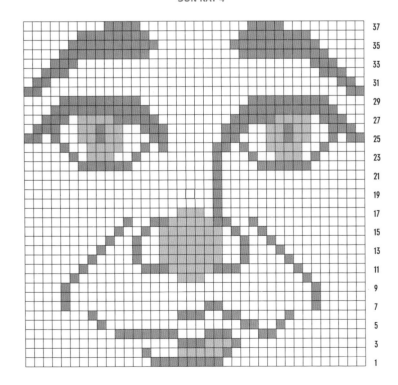

37	
35	
33	
31	
29	
27	
25	
23	
21	
19	
17	
15	
13	
11	
9	
7	
5	
3	
1	

Color Key

☐ 2616 (A)

▨ 2678 (B)

▨ 2661 (C)

☐ center of design; center of block

SUN RAY 5

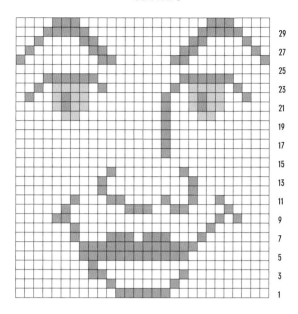

29
27
25
23
21
19
17
15
13
11
9
7
5
3
1

Color Key

☐ 2616 (A)

■ 2678 (B)

▨ 2661 (C)

☐ center of design;
center of block

SUN RAY 6

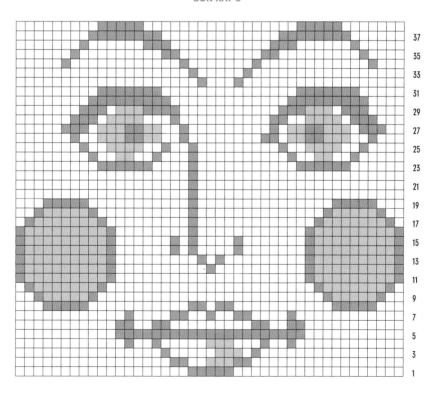

37
35
33
31
29
27
25
23
21
19
17
15
13
11
9
7
5
3
1

Abbreviations

Beg	begin / beginning
Ch	chain
Cn	cable needle
Cont	continue/ continuing
Dec	decrease
Dpn	double pointed needles
Est	established
Foll	follows / following
Hdc	half double crochet
Inc	increase
K	knit
K2tog	knit 2 sts together
Kfb	knit into the front & back of next st
M1	make 1 (increase)
P	purl
P2tog	purl 2 sts together
Pat	pattern
Psso	pass slipped st over
Rem	remain / remaining
Rep	repeat
RS	right side
Sc	single crochet
Skp	slip 1 st, k1 st, pass sl st over k st
Sk2p	slip 1 st, k2tog, pass sl st over k2tog
Sl	slip
Ssk	slip, slip, knit
St	stitch
Tbl	through back loop
WS	wrong side
Wyib	with yarn in back
Wyif	with yarn in front
Yo	yarn over

Crochet Stitches

CHAIN STITCH

1 To make each chain stitch, you need to wrap the yarn over the hook from the back to the front. To do this, keep your index finger straight and twist your wrist toward you. At the same time, twist your other wrist away from you to bring the yarn in front of the hook. Now twist both wrists back to their original positions. The yarn will now be caught under the hook. This is called a yarn over.

2 To draw the yarn through the loop on the hook, first twist your wrist toward you so the hook is facing down. Now pull the yarn through the loop, then twist your wrist back to its original position so the hook is facing you again. You have now made one chain stitch.

3 You might have to adjust the size of the loop on the hook so it slides easily and slightly loosely along the shaft. To make it larger, use the hook to pull up on the loop while allowing the extra yarn needed to feed off your index finger. To make it smaller, use your index finger to pull on the yarn until the loop is the right size. Continue to make chain stitches, adjusting the loop on the hook as you go so all the chain stitches are the same size.

SINGLE CROCHET

  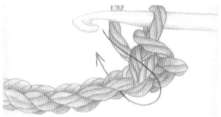

1 Insert the hook under both the front and back loops of the 2nd chain from the hook. (You can also use your other thumb to help it along.) Wrap the yarn over the hook from the back to the front (this is called a yarn over), then catch it with the hook. Now draw the hook through the two chain stitch loops. You now have two loops on the hook.

2 Wrap the yarn over the hook from the back to the front (yarn over), then draw the yarn over through both loops on the hook.

3 You have now completed one single crochet stitch. Continue to repeat Steps 1 and 2 nine more times, inserting the hook into each chain stitch across. You now have ten single crochet stitches completed across the row.

HALF DOUBLE CROCHET

1 Hold the yarn and the crochet hook as before, but for this stitch hold the foundation chain at the 4th chain stitch from the hook. Yarn over the hook from the back to the front. Insert the hook under both the front and back loops of the 3rd chain stitch from the hook. Yarn over the front of the hook and then catch the yarn with the hook. Now draw the hook through the two chain stitch loops. You now have three loops on the hook.

2 Yarn over the hook from the back to the front. Draw the hook through all three loops on the hook.

3 You have now completed one half double crochet stitch. Continue to repeat Steps 1 and 2 nine more times. You now have ten half double crochet stitches completed across the row. To proceed to the next row, make two chain stitches for the turning chain, then turn. Remember that two chain stitches equal the height of the half double crochet. To begin the next row, insert the hook under both the front and back loops of the first stitch (skipping the turning chain stitches). Continue to repeat the steps until you have completed ten rows of half double crochet. Fasten off.

Knitting Techniques

PICKING UP STITCHES

Horizontal edge with knitting needle

Stitches picked up along a bound-off edge.

1 Insert the knitting needle into the center of the first stitch in the row below the bound-off edge. Wrap the yarn knitwise around the needle.

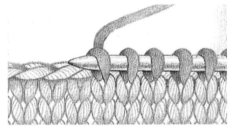

2 Draw the yarn through. You have picked up one stitch. Continue to pick up one stitch in each stitch along the bound-off edge.

Vertical edge with knitting needle

Stitches picked up along a side edge.

1 Insert the knitting needle into the corner stitch of the first row, one stitch in from the side edge. Wrap the yarn around the needle knitwise.

2 Draw the yarn through. You have picked up one stitch. Continue to pick up stitches along the edge. Occasionally skip one row to keep the edge from flaring.

THREE-NEEDLE BIND-OFF
This bind-off is used to join two edges that have the same number of stitches, which have been placed on holders.

1 With the right side of the two pieces facing each other, and the needles parallel, insert a third needle knitwise into the first stitch of each needle. Wrap the yarn around the needle as if to knit.

2 Knit these two stitches together and slip them off the needles. *Knit the next two stitches together in the same way as shown.

3 Slip the first stitch on the third needle over the second stitch and off the needle. Repeat from the * in step 2 across the row until all the stitches are bound off.

WHIP STITCH ON A HEM

Fold the hem to the wrong side, being sure that the stitches are straight. Insert the needle into a stitch on the wrong side of the fabric and then into the cast-on edge of the hem. Draw the yarn through.

I-CORD

Using dpns or a short circular needle, cast on 3 sts or number of stitches required.
Row 1 K3, do not turn, slide sts to other end of needle.
Rep row 1 to desired length. Bind off.

Embroidery Stitches

DUPLICATE STITCH

STRAIGHT STITCH

CHAIN STITCH

FRENCH KNOT

DAISY STITCH

TRELLIS STITCH

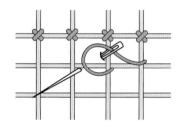

JACOBEAN COUCHING

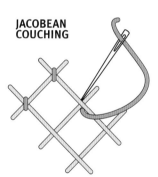

STEM STITCH

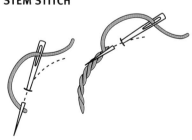

CROSS STITCH

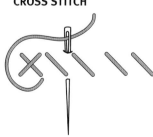

DOUBLE CROSS STITCH

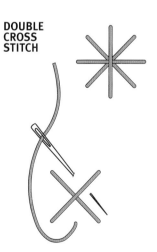

Acknowledgments

I'd like to thank some really wonderful knitters who have been there for me through the years. They worked diligently to help me make some tough editorial deadlines; without them, many of these afghans would still be balls of yarn. In alphabetical order: Jean Bloodgood, Michele Bova, Sue Colistra, Eileen Curry, Nancy Henderson, Daphne McIntyre, Margarita Mejia and Shirley Satler.

Many thanks for the exquisite talent of my art director, Chi Ling Moy; the beautiful photography of Marcus Tullis; and the lovely styling of Laura Maffeo—their efforts captured the unique personality of each afghan.

Thanks to my Sixth&Spring support team...Trisha Malcolm, Art Joinnides, Elaine Silverstein, Erica Smith, Sheena T. Paul, Amanda Keiser, Alan Young, Rachael Stein, David Joinnides and Lillian Esposito.

Special thanks to Vincent Caputo whose amazing artistic ability helped me create many of these afghans.

Thanks and praise to knitters, any and all of you, who have knit or who will knit one of my afghans, and to my students and knitting supporters who have told me that they "take my books to bed with them at night" and use them for "eye candy." Loving thanks to my husband Howard, who refuses to learn how to knit, but can always be counted on to read me a knitting pattern or chart.

And finally, thanks to the "babies"—Scott, Jeff and Ken—whose Grandma Rose knew a thing or two about making beautiful afghans.

Resources

Cascade Yarns
1224 Andover Park East
Tukwila, WA 98188
www.cascadeyarns.com

Classic Elite Yarns
122 Western Avenue
Lowell, MA 01851
www.classiceliteyarns.com

DMC
#10F Port Kearny, South Hackensack Avenue
South Kearny, NJ 07302
www.dmc.com

GGH
distributed by Muench Yarns

Harrisville Designs
Box 806, Center Village
Harrisville, NH 03450
www.harrisville.com

JCA, Inc.
35 Scales Lane
Townsend, MA 01469
www.jcacrafts.com

Lion Brand Yarn
34 West 15th Street
New York, NY 10011
www.lionbrand.com

Muench Yarns, Inc.
1323 Scott Street
Petaluma, CA 94954-1135
www.myyarn.com

Paternayan
distributed by JCA, Inc.

Patons
320 Livingstone Avenue South
Listowel, Ontario
Canada N4W 3H3
www.patonsyarns.com

Reynolds
distributed by JCA, Inc.

Rowan Yarns
4 Townsend West, Unit 8
Nashua, NH 03063
603.886.5041

UK: Green Lane Mill
Holmfirth
HD9 2DX England
+ 44 (0) 1484 681881
www.knitrowan.com

RYC
distributed by Westminster Fibers, Inc.
www.ryclassic.com

Tahki Stacy Charles, Inc.
70-30 80th Street
Building #36
Ridgewood, NY 11385
www.tahkistacycharles.com

Tahki Yarns
distributed by Tahki•Stacy Charles, Inc.

Westminster Fibers
165 Ledge Street
Nashua, NH 03060
www.westminsterfibers.com

Notes

Notes

Notes